The Feng Shui Continuum

The Feng Shui Continuum

A Blueprint for Balanced Living

Kartar Diamond

Four Pillars Publishing

CULVER CITY, CALIFORNIA

DISCLAIMER: Except for the author's representation of herself, the names and identifying characteristics of the people discussed in this book have been changed to protect their privacy. This book is designed to provide accurate and authoritative information in regard to the subject matter covered. It is sold with the understanding that the publisher is not engaged in rendering psychological or other professional services. If expert assistance is needed, the services of a competent professional should be sought.

First printing 2008

ISBN 978-0-9671937-7-9
LCCN 2007935624

ATTENTION CORPORATIONS, UNIVERSITIES, COLLEGES, AND PROFESSIONAL ORGANIZATIONS: Quantity discounts are available on bulk purchases of this book for educational, gift purposes, or as premiums for increasing magazine subscriptions or renewals. Special books or book excerpts can also be created to fit specific needs. For information, please contact Four Pillars Publishing, 3824 Perham Drive, Culver City, CA 90232.

The concept and consciousness of the Teacher is an important theme in my life. I honor all of the various teachers I've had: spiritual teachers, music teachers, martial arts instructors, and teachers I've had in the form of wise friends.

I am especially grateful to Master Sang, a continual source of inspiration. He transcends age and culture and always wants to make everyone around him feel comfortable.

And to my most profound teacher of all, son Nirangkar: May you always shoot for the stars with your feet firmly planted on the ground.

ACKNOWLEDGMENTS

Once again I am indebted to Dr. Lorraine Wilcox, one of the few people who can do content editing for a Feng Shui book. I was also lucky to work again with Lynda Abdo, a fellow consultant, and her daughter Allexis, and thank them for their help with the illustrations.

CONTENTS

Exterior Influences
Use of a Room
The Personal Trigram of the Individuals Using a Space
The East/West School

INTRODUCTION

As the saying goes, "Which came first, the chicken or the egg?" Does the phenomenon of Feng Shui really cause anything to happen in our lives, or is it just a reflection of our predetermined destiny? Do we naturally gravitate toward a living space that will perpetuate our strengths and weaknesses? Or do we have free will with the house really imposing all of its influence upon us? Although I can't answer these questions definitively, I'm inclined to believe that we on Earth are living a combination of free will, karma (an Eastern concept of personal cause and effect that includes reincarnation), *and* the planned or spontaneous influences of our environment.

Questions I can enthusiastically answer are contained in *The Feng Shui Continuum*. Working now with these mystical principles for so many years, I feel confident to share with you how these energies are defined, interpreted, and remedied. *How* and *why* these energies came into being in the first place and with such predictability is anyone's conjecture, however.

It is my sincerest wish that those of you reading this book will consider yourselves part of my global-virtual-classroom, and if there is anything in these pages that confuses you, please contact me via email to discuss it. I am keenly aware of how lucky I was to be spoon-fed this wonderful information by personal instruction with Master Larry Sang. I remember reading one of the few advanced Feng Shui books published many years ago, and I can admit that if I had not already been taught these formulae in the comfort of Master Sang's classroom, my eyes would have glazed over, and I would have struggled with this same material that students worldwide are trying to learn just through books or through Internet courses. Not everyone is as lucky as I to have a Feng Shui Grand Master living just thirty minutes away. And not everyone is as lucky as I to have a steady stream of opportunities to test and prove the theories contained in this book.

Good luck to you always, and here's to even better luck with the help of Feng Shui!

Kartar Diamond

CHAPTER ONE

Thank Your Lucky Stars

INTRODUCTION TO FENG SHUI AND THE FLYING STARS

I've never met a person who did not want to improve his or her health, have more energy, and relate better to friends, family, lovers, and co-workers. I've never met anyone who did not want to improve his or her financial status or at least ensure that it be maintained. I include myself in those same desires and goals, so you can imagine how excited I got when I first discovered Feng Shui in 1990. Here we have an ancient system that not only diagnoses some of the causes of our challenges and setbacks, but also provides answers to how we can improve those circumstances and have more affluence, health, and love in our lives. Both the causes and the solutions can be found in our immediate physical surroundings.

Feng Shui has historically been a somewhat cloistered subject and not readily available to just anyone who wanted to learn it. But now much of that has changed. If Feng Shui is about being at the right place at the right time, then anyone with access to this wisdom must already have a little bit of good Feng Shui working for them.

Feng Shui can be described in a few of my favorite phrases:

- Astrology for architecture (because of the similar coordinates of time and location needed to define the "personality" or potential influence of the space).
- Acupuncture for the home (because of the concepts of energy flow and balance).
- The metaphysical interpretation of your environment (because this is still uncharted territory for the Western scientific world).
- The predictable influences of time and space on people and nature (because Feng Shui is one aspect of the space-time continuum).

Feng Shui is a vast body of knowledge, with the documentation of it beginning in China thousands of years ago and with a rich history throughout Asia. But how does that relate to you, on whatever continent you reside, in the here and now? I am always trying to keep practical application at the forefront of my agenda when writing about Feng Shui for the masses. Feng Shui is as relevant and applicable today as it has ever been. And you can pronounce it:

- fung shway
- feng shoo'ee
- fung shoy
- foong sway
- or fang shih, to name a few.

Feng (wind) shui (water) is about dissecting your surroundings and observing how they influence you. It is a system for showcasing the predictability of how people interact with nature as well as man-made surroundings.

Sometimes you can even see through Feng Shui analysis how God (the Creator of all) has a sense of humor! As an example, there is actually a house type and floor plan that can reveal whether the man in the house will be bald! Many Feng Shui coincidences are downright funny.

Now, to be sure, I never thought I would put "God" and "Feng Shui" in the same sentence, because I have spent exorbitant amounts of time lecturing about how Feng Shui is not a religion. Nor is it part and parcel of any Buddhist practices, even though it comes from a culture and land where more people practice Buddhism than any other religion. It is not a belief system, but rather a *near* science, because enough variables can be repeated to predict a similar outcome when all those known variables converge.

But once a year or so I get a piece of hate mail from someone who wants to scold me about how Feng Shui is bogus and not based on any scientific evidence whatsoever. This often comes from someone without a scientific background, I can assure you. And I tend to remind these folks that in order to have a truly scientific mind, one must keep his or her mind *open and objective* for discovery.

Of course, Feng Shui is not scientific by any Western standards— not yet. But sometimes I have to remind people that the "science" of the day keeps changing. Just look at our health and diet industry as one small example. In the mid-1990s there was a woman named Susan Powter who wrote a bestseller called *Stop the Insanity.* She told people that if they wanted to lose fat they should just stop eating fat! Pretty simple, right? She had devotees trying to lose weight by stuffing themselves with fat-free carbohydrates. Meanwhile, less than ten years later, American culture coined a new phrase "carb-phobic" because millions of people went back to the Dr. Atkins concept of avoiding carbohydrates for large portions of protein and fat instead. And a whole new generation of skinny people with clogged arteries and colons emerged. As I write this book, the diet pendulum is swinging back again to the "Mediterranean diet," in vogue for the umpteenth time. I can find many examples of how subjective and revolving "the science of the day" really is, especially with regard to even more serious matters related to health and longevity. But that is not what this book is about. And this is not a Feng Shui Fad Diet book, like so many that were published years ago, with authors literally making stuff up as they went along. This book is about a time-tested system that evolved over thousands of years and that truly works for most of the people, most of the time.

QI-FLOW AND FORM SCHOOL
VERSUS FLYING STARS

A big part of Feng Shui has nothing to do, at first glance, with timing or direction. All Feng Shui schools concern themselves with something called qi-flow. Qi is pronounced like "chee." Qi is energy, matter, life force, air currents. The flow of interior energies is partly based on qualities that we can later define as "yin" or "yang," as well as the dimensions of a room and the arrangement of furnishings. As an example, if a person wants to walk from point A to point B and there is a couch in between, the person needs to walk around the couch or at least jump over it. You cannot walk through it. As well, the qi (air currents) in a room will also circulate around, under, or over the furnishings. But unlike people and animals, qi can also move right through physical objects, including walls. Qi can be *partly* contained, and it moves *less* freely through solid areas, such as walls, yet it can still permeate all spaces to some degree. And we as human beings are actually quite porous, too, because we can absorb the qi in a room, breathe it in, as well as produce our own qi.

Qi will flow along beams and baseboards, around corners, and bounce off furnishings. One goal in Feng Shui is to arrange physical items in a room in a way that will create a smooth and harmonious flow of qi, as opposed to jarring irregular movement. That said, we are mostly concerned with fairly large pieces of furniture or architectural features. In other words, you do not need to obsess over the positioning of a paperweight on your desk.

And all of this is done in order to enhance our health, well-being, and prosperity potential. There is a real connection between how well or how poorly energy flows around us and how well or how poorly we do in our lives.

The vast majority of English-language Feng Shui books printed in the last two decades of the twentieth century focused on qi-flow. Not only are interiors checked for harmonious qi-flow, but exterior influences can be categorized as creating a good or bad flow or just emanating good or bad energy. Good energy is sometimes referred to as "sheng qi," and bad energy is sometimes referred to as "sha qi."

Sha qi can literally move, such as the chaotic, frenzied air currents generated from traffic on a freeway. But sha qi can also appear fairly still, such as something that is ugly to look at, like a billboard sign with a depressing message. And to that extent, sheng qi or sha qi can sometimes be subjective. There will be objective circumstances that affect all people similarly, and there will also be subjective interpretations of an environment.

Form School includes the study of natural landscapes. One way to identify the best spot is to look for what is different among things that are the same. For example, if you have a series of tall mountains and then a significantly lower open space, that is often considered the place where the sheng qi collects.

FIGURE 1A

Here is an illustration of a mountain range, and where there is a gap of open space, the sheng qi collects.

Conversely, if you have a large span of flat land and then all of a sudden a mountain pops up, that mountainous eruption could also indicate a probable location for the pooling of sheng qi.

FIGURE 1B

Here is an illustration of a flat area and then an isolated mountain popping up.

The Flying Stars are one type of qi. The Flying Stars are part of the energetic fabric of any given interior space. Flying Stars are mutable and moveable energies that also influence exterior spaces, but the emphasis in this book will be how they congregate in interior spaces.

These Flying Stars are a manifestation of time and space. Calculations can be performed on any enclosure based on its orientation and year of construction, and a "Flying Star chart" can be produced and interpreted for its effect on the occupants of that space. And that is the emphasis of this book—to create a Flying Star chart and then enable the reader to interpret it. You can imagine that it is like a type of energy grid sitting right inside any floor plan.

WHY THE FLYING STARS ARE SO IMPORTANT

The Flying Stars are such a big topic, having so many layers, that it is impossible to cover the full scope of it in an ordinary sized book. In my previous books, I highlighted isolated applications of the Flying

Stars, such as Annual Cycles. But the Annual Cycles have much more meaning when compared to or grouped with the permanent energies of a space.

Qi-flow, sheng qi, and sha qi will interact with the Flying Stars, which are also their own type of sheng qi and sha qi. As an example, a dark dingy entrance can make a person feel depressed or lower his or her energy upon entering. If this environment is coupled with a "Flying Star 2," it will make that space even worse because the Flying Star 2 by itself can attract loneliness or sickness, even in a space that otherwise appears bright and cheery. You will learn in this book about how these numbers, *as codes for energy* and also referred to as Stars, will influence so many aspects of your life.

All aspects of Feng Shui are important, including Form School principles, which note how air currents travel through a space, the shapes and dimensions of the architecture and the furnishings, yin-yang features (opposites and extremes), and natural exterior surroundings. But this book will focus on the Flying Stars first and then on their relation to everything else.

Before launching into the Flying Stars, I do want to emphasize that the overall environment is quite important, in case someone who has not read my other books should think I am neglecting these other essential principles. The overall environment is especially influential because it often includes features you cannot change, like a mountainside near your house or a design flaw in a house you are only renting. But what I have found is that absolutely everyone is affected by the Flying Stars, whereas not everyone has seriously bad environmental features to deal with. *In fact, most environments are rather ordinary.* So learning the Flying Stars is very practical and valuable for both the lay person and the aspiring professional. It is like putting on a pair of X-ray vision glasses that allow you to see what no one else can.

Serious Feng Shui practitioners will need to learn about every possible flaw that can exist in an environment and, if there is a remedy, try to test it out personally or recommend it to others. Like a doctor who must study even the rarest of diseases so he or she can recognize it if one patient in a lifetime has that problem, so too must a Feng Shui course of study include the less frequent or even obscure problems.

Here is an example: An exceedingly long, straight walkway to a house can be a problem in how it directs the qi (air currents) toward a front door. The longer the qi moves in a straight line, the more harmful the energy can become. The result is that the occupants inside the house could have any variety of problems. And yet, in all my years in practice, I may only have seen an exceedingly long walkway a handful of times. *Compare that to 100% of the population who have to deal with the effects of the Flying Stars on a regular basis.*

- Living at the bottom of a canyon is not good "Form School" environmental Feng Shui, but I bet that hardly any of you reading this book have this problem.

- Living in a house that teeters off the edge of a cliff is a formidable problem, though rare.

- And how many of you live across the street from an airport runway? Hardly any of you or just a tiny percentage, I am sure.

- And yet, 100% of you have the Flying Stars residing in your homes and businesses.

- 100% of you can also benefit from enhancing the good Flying Stars that engender creativity, health, and wealth, and 100% of you can benefit from diminishing the power of the negative Flying Stars.

So, to summarize, there are countless Form School situations and countless environmental concerns that one can have, but the reality is that most of us do not have to contend with really extreme environmental situations. Here are a few more examples:

- How many of you live in a building shaped like a triangle? Not so good, but not common either.

- How many of you live with oppressively low ceilings? Not so many.

- But 100% of you are affected by these invisible bundles of energy that we call the Flying Stars.

I have been to a few places with Master Sang where he has said to students, "Don't even bother pulling out your compasses." And I have certainly seen a hundred of these kinds of places on my own. Some environments are so horrible that we don't even care what the Flying Stars are. But is that you and your circumstances? *Probably not.* So, let us begin the journey of discovering what these Flying Stars are and how to harness them to our benefit. Once you get a working knowledge of the Flying Stars, you will be amazed at how accurately they reflect what has happened to you in the past. And then you can get even more excited about controlling your present and future.

CHAPTER TWO

How to Create a Flying Star Chart

DRAW AN ACCURATE FLOOR PLAN

It is imperative to draw a decent floor plan sketch of your home or business, since a major component to Feng Shui is dealing with real divisions of physical space. At the very least, you need to get graph paper, measuring tape, or other measuring devices and make a reduction of your floor plan. You don't want to reduce the size so much that it is hard to look at on paper, but you do want to make it small enough that it is manageable to work with on ordinary-sized paper instead of blueprints. As an example, if you measure out a room to be 12 square feet, you can reduce it to 4 square centimeters or 2 square inches on a piece of paper. Just decide for yourself if you want half an inch to equal three or four feet or a centimeter to equal three or four feet. Homes that are under 2,500 square feet can often be fully represented on an 8½″ by 11″ letter-sized piece of paper. Two-story homes are best done on two pieces of paper.

Start with a room that is in one corner of the house. Measure it out, draw it, and then proceed to another adjacent room and keep connecting the rooms. You do not have to measure down to a fraction of an inch or even obsess about wall width, unless the walls are very thick, which is the case with some styles of architecture.

To get good at drawing floor plans takes practice. But if you are only trying to evaluate your own living space, then take your time and make it a project.

If this task seems utterly impossible for you, then find a person with some design or drafting background to help you. Some of my long-distance clients have hired a local architect or designer to come over and draw out their plan for them, but this is usually not necessary. Most people can draw a good sketch themselves if they take the time.

DIVIDE UP THE SECTORS OF THE FLOOR PLAN

A floor plan is divided up into nine sections like a tic-tac-toe square. You will take the floor plan and divide it up into equal divisions of thirds, both in terms of length and width. After drawing a to-scale floor plan sketch, you can see the real shape of your home, which is most likely some version of a square or rectangle. Some floor plans will have a missing section or a partially missing section or two. Some floor plans will reveal an extension. The nine-area grid is referred to as a *luo shu grid,* which is superimposed over your floor plan.

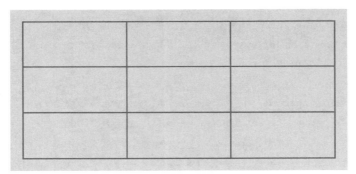

FIGURE 2A

A luo shu grid is the nine-area grid superimposed over all floor plans. It will cover most, if not all, floor plans. Above is Fig. 2A, a rectangular shaped luo shu grid.

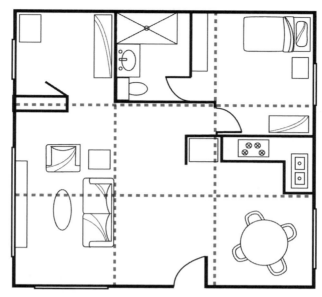

In FIGURE 2B you can see a nine-area luo shu grid superimposed over a simple floor plan.

Each one of the nine areas is a distinct directional area, which can be referred to as a "section," a "sector," or a Chinese term translated as a "palace." In my other books I referred to each of these sectors as "quadrants." If the location of East were being discussed, it could be called the East section, the East sector, the East palace, or the East quadrant. Some people refer to a directional area as a "cell" or a "zone." It should be understood that they are all interchangeable terms that refer to 1/9th of the luo shu grid.

You do not want to end up with more than 1 to 1 ½ missing sectors for the whole plan. If you end up with too much missing space, then you need to shrink your luo shu grid down, and you will then end up with some extensions instead. An extension is just more of the same area it is attached to.

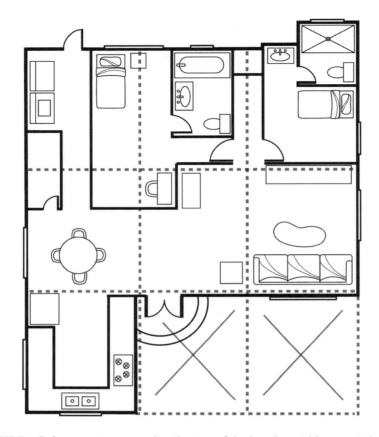

FIGURE 2C shows an improper distribution of the luo shu grid because it leaves open too much missing space.

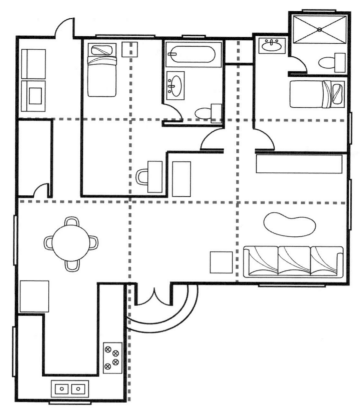

FIGURE 2D. The same floor plan as in Fig. 2C is shown in Fig. 2D with the proper distribution of the luo shu grid.

You can thumb through other chapters in this book that have examples of floor plans showing the directional divisions to help you understand the way you should divide up your own space.

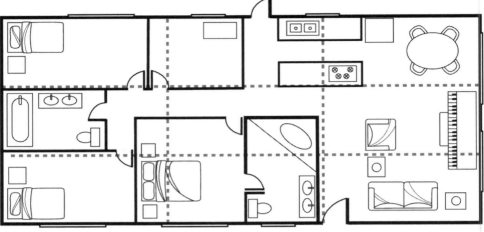

FIGURE 2E shows a rectangular-shaped house with a luo shu grid over it.

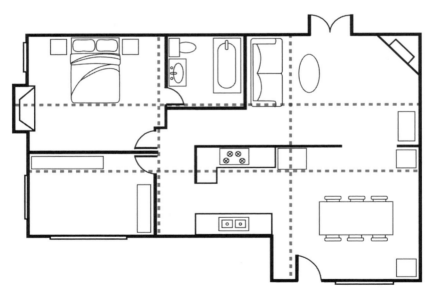

FIGURE 2F is a rectangular-shaped house with an extension, showing the luo shu grid over it.

WHY YOU NEED TO TAKE A COMPASS READING

You literally need to go out and buy a good quality compass and take a reading in front of your property and *not* just assume that your house or building faces a certain direction. Every 15 degrees there is another type of house orientation, and you cannot just make an estimate. It needs to be verified with a compass, especially since some properties sit very close to the cut-off points of different directions.

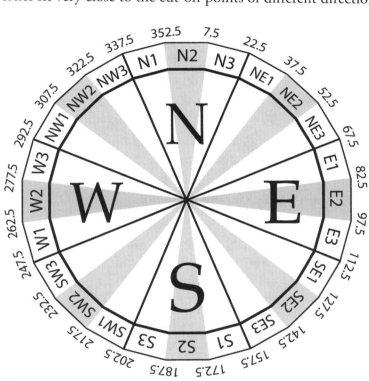

FIGURE 2G is an illustration of a compass showing all 360 degrees, with the 24 different 15-degree sectors.

In a Feng Shui analysis:

- We *do not* determine the direction a house faces based on the location or movement of the sun.
- We *do not* use True North as a reference either, which is why looking at street maps is usually not good enough. Not every structure is aligned perfectly parallel with a street, either.

- When you look at a map, there will usually be a True North arrow located somewhere on the edge of the map to give you a True North reference. But what you need to know is the *magnetic reading*, which varies from place to place. If you want to learn more about magnetic declinations, just Google the words, and you will be taken to some informative sites.

- Architectural drawings often show a "north" sign on the blueprint, but they could easily just be an estimate and not even reliable as a True North indicator.

- A geological survey map can show either True North or Magnetic North, so you would want to get that verified by whoever did the site survey.

- Satellite photos on the Internet sites Mapquest.com, Zillow.com, Terraserver.com, and Google Earth will show an aerial photo with True North at the top edge of your computer screen. You will then want to know what the magnetic declination is for that area, as a comparison, if you are trying to evaluate a property you have not visited in person.

- What *we do* use in Feng Shui is the magnetic compass reading, which could be east or west of True North by anywhere from 0 to 18 degrees depending on where you live.

For example, in Los Angeles, California, Magnetic North is presently 13 degrees *east* of True North. If you were looking at a street map and it appeared as though a house in Los Angeles would be facing exactly 90 degrees East, it would in fact be closer to 77 degrees Magnetic East. (90 degrees *minus* 13 degrees = 77 degrees.)

In Manhattan, New York, Magnetic North is presently 12 degrees *west* of True North. If you were looking at a street map for Manhattan and it appeared that a house was facing exactly 90 degrees East, it would instead be closer to102 degrees. (90 degrees *plus* 12 degrees for this magnetic variation.)

HOW TO TAKE A COMPASS READING

You can use a traditional luo pan (Chinese Feng Shui compass) or you can use a regular Western compass. I use the Cammenga military compass available online or at your local Army-Navy surplus store. Just make sure your compass is good quality. As a comparison, I have seen junky toy-like luo pans being sold on eBay for hardly anything whereas some good-quality luo pans will cost several hundred dollars. Likewise, with Western compasses, you could pick up a little $15 compass at a camping store, but the better-quality compasses will be $50 or more. I recommend the compasses you can get at the Army-Navy surplus stores, and, of course, you can peruse the Internet. Once you have your good-quality compass that shows every single degree on its dial, stand parallel to the *facing side* (what you consider to be the front side) of the house or building and hold your compass parallel to the property and level with the ground. The compass arrow will move around and within seconds point to where Magnetic North is (0 degrees). If you are using a Chinese compass designed for Feng Shui analysis (the luo pan), then the arrow will point to Magnetic South (180 degrees).

Why is the Chinese Feng Shui compass designed to point to South? The direction of South is associated with "yang" qualities, like movement and growth and summertime and is considered generally a more desirable direction than North, which is associated with dormancy, death, and winter. Historically, the Chinese map will place South on the top of the page because of this cultural preference. This is how the Feng Shui myth of South being a lucky direction got started. But there is nothing lucky or unlucky about any direction. It is simply not enough information to go on. If your compass is not a luo pan, it will not clearly show the cut of points or divisions between the designated 24 Chinese directions. Refer to the following chart:

Compass chart showing cut-off points for the 24 Directions

Directions/ Abbreviations	Degree Ranges
North 1 (N1)	337.5–352.5
North 2 (N2)	352.5–7.5
North 3 (N3)	7.5–22.5
Northeast 1 (NE1)	22.5–37.5
Northeast 2 (NE2)	37.5–52.5
Northeast 3 (NE3)	52.5–67.5
East 1 (E1)	67.5–82.5
East 2 (E2)	82.5–97.5
East 3 (E3)	97.5–112.5
Southeast 1 (SE1)	112.5–127.5
Southeast 2 (SE2)	127.5–142.5
Southeast 3 (SE3)	142.5–157.5
South 1 (S1)	157.5–172.5
South 2 (S2)	172.5–187.5
South 3 (S3)	187.5–202.5
Southwest 1 (SW1)	202.5–217.5
Southwest 2 (SW2)	217.5–232.5
Southwest 3 (SW3)	232.5–247.5
West 1 (W1)	247.5–262.5
West 2 (W2)	262.5–277.5
West 3 (W3)	277.5–292.5
Northwest 1 (NW1)	292.5–307.5
Northwest 2 (NW2)	307.5–322.5
Northwest 3 (NW3)	322.5–337.5

FIGURE 2H shows a person standing in front of a house, holding a compass.

Some compasses have a silhouette of an arrow in the center. You need to shift a dial on that type of compass so that the real arrow is inside the silhouette. That will get your compass arrow pointing to 0 on the perimeter of your compass.

On other compasses the arrow is attached to the dial, which will shift automatically to point to North, and then you will see what direction is in front of you and behind you in relation to where North is.

If you stand facing a house and the North arrow points directly toward the back of the house, it means the house "sits" to the North. In other words, the back wall is a North wall.

If you stand facing a house and the North arrow points directly to the right of your body, then that direction is North, thus making the back of the house the West direction, which should be evident when you look down at your compass.

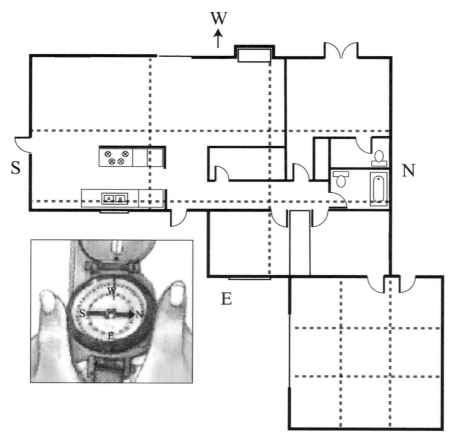

FIGURE 2I compares the compass reading with posting the correct directions on each side of the house.

- Always stand exactly parallel to a property when doing a reading.
- Stand ten to twenty feet away from the front wall.
- Make sure you are not near any heavy metal objects, like a car.
- Do a comparative compass reading on the back side of the property to make sure your readings are consistent.
- If the compass needle is really wavering and you do not get a consistent reading on the front and back side, then you have to make sure you are not standing too close to metal. Of course, it is entirely possible that a front wall might not be exactly parallel to a back wall.

- With square or rectangular structures, the back side should be just about 180 degrees opposite the front side. For example, a house that faces North should be sitting South. A house that faces West should be sitting East. Not every structure is a box, however.

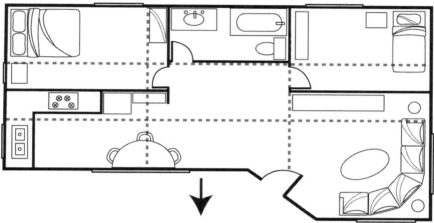

FIGURE 2J shows a house with an angled front wall.

The house with an angled wall is still facing, technically, the exact opposite direction of the sitting side. It is like a person's body. Your chest faces the opposite direction from your back; however, if your head is turned at an angle, then it will not be parallel to the chest or back. Someone turning his or her head is like a house with an angled façade.

IMPORTANT FOOTNOTE ABOUT COMPASS READINGS

If you are trying to evaluate a property long distance, using aerial photos and maps, it is essential to find out what the magnetic declination is for that area. The National Geophysical Data Center website has a page where you can just plug in the zip code for anywhere in the United States and find what the magnetic declination is for that area. And just so you know, the magnetic declination does not change very much within a city. In fact, it might be the same declination for a major swath of area spanning fifty or more miles.

For example, from Los Angeles County to Orange County (a span of fifty to eighty miles) it changes by only 1 degree.

If you are trying to figure out the magnetic declination of an area outside the United States, you can go to Google Earth first to locate the property or general area. It will also show you the longitude and latitude for that area on the bottom of the aerial view. You can jot down that information, go back to the National Geophysical Data Center website, and plug in the longitude and latitude number coordinates to find the magnetic declination.

For example, the longitude and latitude coordinates in London, England, are 51 degrees North and 0 degrees West, which translates as a magnetic declination 1 degree West of True North. So for London, Magnetic North and True North are presently almost the same.

The longitude and latitude coordinates in Tokyo, Japan, are 35 degrees North and 139 degrees East, which translates to Magnetic North being 6 degrees West of True North. If you look at a map of Tokyo for a building that appears to face exactly North, a person standing with a compass at that location would get a reading of facing 6 degrees instead of 0 degrees from his or her compass.

The longitude and latitude for Dallas, Texas, is 32 degrees North and 96 degrees West. Plug those coordinates into the National Geophysical Data Center calculator and you find that Magnetic North in Dallas is 4 degrees east of True North.

With the help of the Internet we can now find out the magnetic declination of anywhere in the world. You may wonder why we use Magnetic North as a reference in Feng Shui instead of True North. The type of qi we are diagnosing in Feng Shui is calculated by the local magnetic energies of the area.

The actual website address for the National Geophysical Data Center might change after the publication of this book, so just Google the words "National Geophysical Data Center," and you should be able to locate it. I am sure there are other websites that can give you this information as well.

IDENTIFY THE DIRECTIONAL SECTORS ON THE FLOOR PLAN

Once you have done your compass reading and have your accurate floor plan sketch in front of you, then you can note on your floor plan the division of the directional sectors and correctly identify them on the plan.

If the house faces Northeast, you can post the abbreviation for Northeast (NE) inside or near the facing sector on the plan. Then you can proceed to fill in the rest of the sectors with their correct directional designation.

Example 1: Here is an example of a Northeast-facing rectangular-shaped space with the Northeast side facing toward the top of the page. The symbol (^) will designate the facing side throughout this book, and in some cases the "V" sign will show a facing side toward the bottom of a page.

^

N	N	E
NW		SE
W	SW	S

Example 2: Here is an example of a Northeast-facing space with the Northeast side facing toward the *bottom* of the page. You can draw a floor plan or luo shu grid either way. It is just an aerial view.

S	SW	W
SE		NW
E	NE	N

V

CONSTRUCTION PERIOD OF THE HOUSE

Every house and building has been constructed within a certain era or Construction Period. These Periods are twenty years in length. Each Period begins on February 4th within these twenty-year Periods because February 4th is the midpoint between the Winter Solstice and the Spring Equinox. (It should not be confused with the Chinese Lunar Calendar, which vacillates from year to year.)

These twenty-year Periods repeat every 180 years because we have nine Periods lasting for twenty years each.

Period 1: February 4th 1864 to February 3rd 1884

Period 2: February 4th 1884 to February 3rd 1904

Period 3: February 4th 1904 to February 3rd 1924

Period 4: February 4th 1924 to February 3rd 1944

Period 5: February 4th 1944 to February 3rd 1964

Period 6: February 4th 1964 to February 3rd 1984

Period 7: February 4th 1984 to February 3rd 2004

Period 8: February 4th 2004 to February 3rd 2024

Period 9: February 4th 2024 to February 3rd 2044

Period 1: February 4th 2044 to February 3rd 2064

Period 2: February 4th 2064 to February 3rd 2084

Period 3: February 4th 2084 to February 3rd 2104

Period 4: February 4th 2104 to February 3rd 2124

Period 5: February 4th 2124 to February 3rd 2144

Period 6: February 4th 2144 to February 3rd 2164

Period 7: February 4th 2164 to February 3rd 2184

Period 8: February 4th 2184 to February 3rd 2204

Period 9: February 4th 2204 to February 3rd 2224

CHARTING THE PERIOD STAR

You need to know when your house or building was built. If you don't know, and the property is not more than one hundred years old, then there should be some official record of the year of construction with either the tax assessor's office or the department of building and safety in your local area. Some of this information is now online and easy to access. Even in the United States there are some buildings that are quite old, and sometimes the age of the building is well known because of its historical significance. A Feng Shui practitioner named Monica Hess once sent me a copy of her little book called *The Feng Shui of George Washington's Mount Vernon*. It would be quite fascinating and quite laborious to study the effects of any well-known buildings over decades or centuries. But this is exactly how Feng Shui has been documented.

Please do verify when your house or apartment building was built with actual records and do not make assumptions or take the landlord's estimate as the last word. People who do not realize how important this information is for Feng Shui purposes will unintentionally make estimates that could prove to be wrong. If someone thinks his or her house was built in 1943 and it proves to have been built just one year later, in 1944, then the house was built in Period 5, not Period 4. Also, a building or house could be completely remodeled inside and appear quite new, but it will still resonate with its original Construction Period. The criteria for determining when a house is considered built or finished is based on when the ceiling is enclosed. A house is built over months or years. When the ceiling and roof go on, that seals the energy in the house, and that is the year to take note of, even if other features of the house are not yet completed.

What is more challenging is finding out when additions have been built. Sometimes people build a room onto a house without getting construction permits. Undocumented additions such as these are more difficult to diagnose. This frustrates Feng Shui consultants much the same way an astrologer is limited if someone does not have his or her exact time of birth.

Once you have determined the Period during which your house was built, place the number associated with that Period in the very center "palace" of your floor plan. I am going to refer to the center sector as a "palace."

So, if your house was built in Period 4, then place the number 4 in the center palace. Example: a house built between February 1924 and February 1944 is a Period 4 House.

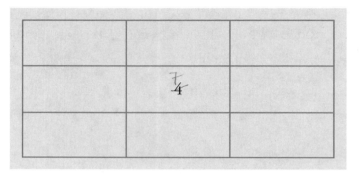

Once you have placed the Period Star in the center palace, you are then going to continue placing succeeding numbers in the other directional sectors, and the numbers (which are called Stars) will follow two consistent patterns.

- The Period Star succession will always *ascend* until you get to the number 9, and then you will start over with the number 1.

- The *location* of where you ascend these Stars/numbers will always follow the same pattern of moving from the center to the Northwest to West to Northeast to South to North to Southwest to East and then to Southeast. This is a pattern that you just have to memorize.

In a Period 4 house, if the number ascends and the direction after the center is Northwest, then you will place a number 5 in the Northwest sector of your house. Continuing along with these two patterns, if the next number has to be 6 and the next direction is West, you will jot down the number 6 in the West sector of your floor plan.

T/A   *Family*   *Guest bottom*   *Bathroom*

SE *3-4* *Nook* 3 6	S *7-8* 8 2	SW *5-6* 1 4
E *4-5* *kitchen* 2 5	Center *2-3* 4 7	W *9-1* 6 9
NE *8-9* 7 1	N *6-7* 9 3	NW *1-2* 5 8

Bedroom

Guest   *Dining*

With the chart above, we can say that the house might face any particular direction. At this point, we are not concerned. We just want to "float" the Period Star in the correct sequence numerically and directionally.

If this house chart happens to be facing North, (like the chart with North towards bottom of the page) then the North sector has the number 9 in it for a Period 4 House and the North sector would be referred to as the *facing sector or the facing palace.*

If this house chart is facing South (toward top of page), then the South sector has the number 8 for this same Period 4 House, and the South sector is referred to as the *facing sector* or the *facing palace* and the North is considered the *sitting sector* or *sitting palace.* The sitting and facing palaces are opposite directions.

If this Period 4 House faces West, we would see that the Period Star in the West sector would be 6. The Period Star in the sitting palace (East) would be 2.

Another example:

E 5	SE 6	S 2
NE 1	Center 7	SW 4
N 3	NW 8	W 9

Here we have a house that was built in Period 7, so the number 7 is placed in the center palace. Sometimes people are used to seeing North on the top of a directional example and South on the bottom, but you need to *get used to seeing the directions displayed in other ways*, and you can always just think of it like an aerial view.

We can look at the above example and visualize a real house that faces Northwest (with the Northwest wall parallel to the bottom of this page and the Southeast wall parallel with the top of this page).

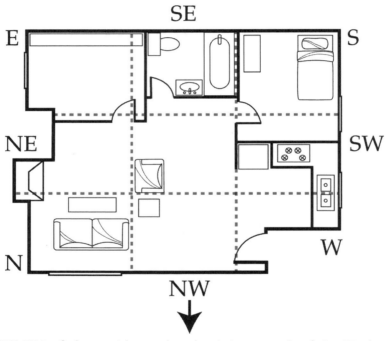

FIGURE 2K is of a house with several partly missing sectors but facing Northwest with the luo shu grid superimposed over it.

The same general rules are still in force with this house type, as compared with the first example of a Period 4 chart. First, you will *ascend* the numbers, continuing with the number 8 following the Period 7 number in the center. And the exact same pattern of NW, W, NE, S, N, SW, E, and SE is in effect for "floating the numbers," which is also called "Flying the Stars." Check this pattern right now with the above chart to make sure you understand the sequencing of the numbers with the directional pattern.

Period Star Chart

Below is a chart that shows the 9 Periods at the top of each column and then the location of where to plot the succeeding Numbers/Stars in each direction. This can be your reference chart to make sure you are floating the Period Stars correctly. If you do not float this Period Star correctly, then *all* your other calculations might be incorrect.

Period	1	2	3	4	5	6	7	8	9
Center	1	2	3	4	5	6	7	8	9
NW	2	3	4	5	6	7	8	9	1
W	3	4	5	6	7	8	9	1	2
NE	4	5	6	7	8	9	1	2	3
S	5	6	7	8	9	1	2	3	4
N	6	7	8	9	1	2	3	4	5
SW	7	8	9	1	2	3	4	5	6
E	8	9	1	2	3	4	5	6	7
SE	9	1	2	3	4	5	6	7	8

DETERMINING THE SITTING AND FACING OF THE STRUCTURE

After dividing up your floor plan into directional sectors, it now becomes essential to understand what is the sitting side of the house (back side) and what is the facing side of the house (front side). This is not always obvious because the main entrance door side is not always on the facing side of the dwelling.

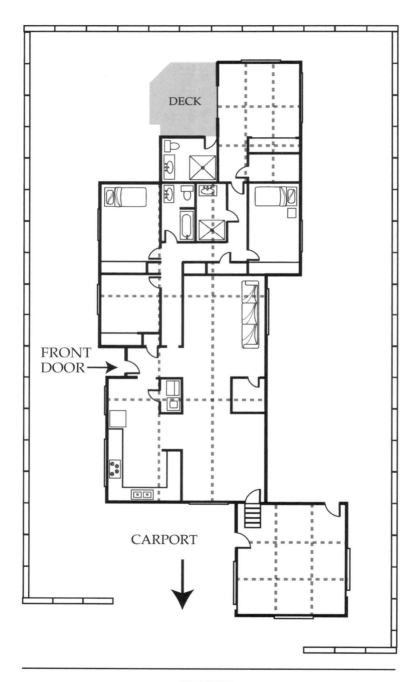

FIGURE 2L shows a front door on the side of the house, but the house faces the street side.

Whole courses can be taught regarding non-obvious orientations, but for the purposes of this book, the general guidelines you should follow are these:

The more "yang" side of the structure is almost always the facing side, and the more "yin" side of the structure is almost always the sitting side. It is possible that the facing side of a house could be more yin, once in a great while. A house's sitting and facing aspects could become confusing when the architect or builder disregards basic principles or good design; it does happen every now and then.

The principles of Yin-Yang theory can be applied to many other aspects of Feng Shui. For example, a river bed that hardly ever has water in it can have a "yin" quality to it (stillness) while a street that is heavily used (active) could be called "yang." A desert is considered a yin environment whereas a lush landscape could be considered more yang.

The Tai Ji or Yin-Yang Symbol shows a division of black and white within the circle to symbolize the yin (feminine) and the yang (masculine). The dot in each section shows that there is yin in yang and vice versa. Yin-Yang theory pervades Chinese metaphysics, Chinese medicine and martial arts, and, of course, Feng Shui.

FIGURE 2M shows the Tai Ji Symbol in its most proper placement, with the yang side on the top.

For determining what the front side is and what the back side is, here are some guidelines:

Examples of Yang Features

- Biggest rooms
- Best view or only view
- Biggest windows (windows are like eyes)
- The most active side of structure: traffic, ocean, etc.
- Warmest side, brightest side
- Most open rooms or spaces
- Lower land level with unobstructed views

Examples of Yin Features

- Smallest rooms
- No views or limited views
- Solid walls (like a back for support)
- The quietest side, least activity
- Coolest, darkest side
- More clustering of smaller spaces, especially plumbing (like bathrooms and kitchens in apartment buildings)
- Higher land level, including a real mountain right next to a house

There are many instances where a main door can actually be on the side of the house or even on the sitting side, so that is why I have not listed the main door in either the yin or yang categories. In apartment living, often the one entrance is from a common internal hallway (sitting side) while the windows to the apartment and the only views are on the opposite side (facing).

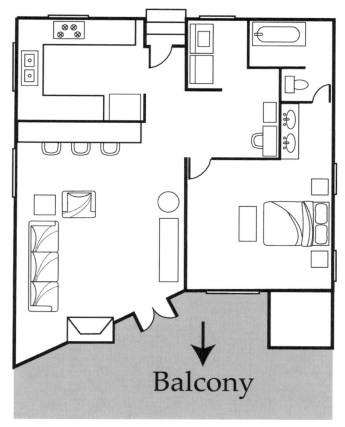

FIGURE 2N is of an apartment with facing side toward the balcony.

In older structures, bedrooms and kitchens were usually in the back/ sitting side of the house. But that is no longer a guideline to trust. Especially with apartment living, bedrooms are often on the facing side in tandem with a living room while the rooms that require plumbing all line the opposite side of the apartment.

Corner units can be confusing when they have competing views from different sides.

By comparing attached apartments and by process of elimination, one can usually figure out the sitting and facing for non-obvious orientations, although even experienced practitioners can be challenged by unconventional design layouts.

The street address is not always the indicator of what direction a house or building faces. Sometimes the structure is turned away from the street side, so just the address could be misleading.

The floor plan in Fig. 20 reveals a non-obvious orientation. It has yin features on both the North side and the West side. The North side is the conventional backyard, and there is a much higher land level, a real hill. The West side has a row of bedrooms.

As well, the South side and the East side have competing yang features. The South side is the street side with a lot of sun and a lower land level. The East side is where the garage, the front door, and another side entrance are located.

Ultimately, it is the outside environment that is the deal breaker with this case study. This house sits North and faces South.

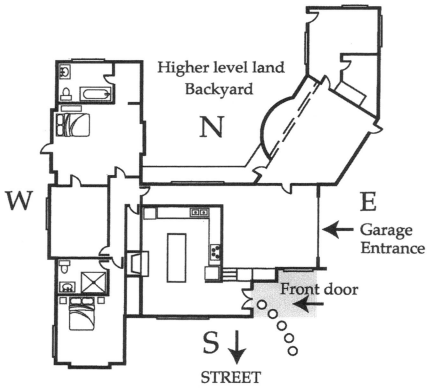

FIGURE 20

Just as there are rules, there are also exceptions to the rules. Next is a floor plan of a house where the facing side has determined not only the orientation, but also the unusual placement of the luo shu grid. It is rare for the sitting side of a property to come to a point, especially for residential structures. Almost always, the sitting side is a flat side and the longest side, but there are rare exceptions. In Fig. 2P, the facing side of this house is mostly glass and was designed completely to take advantage of the views. The facing side is also longer than any of the other exterior walls.

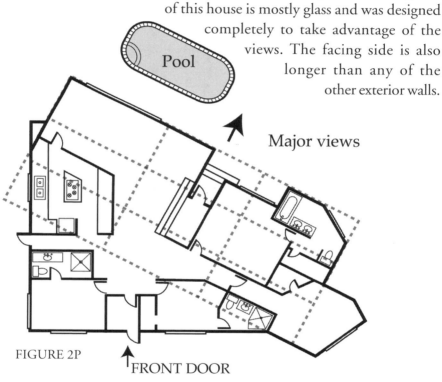

FIGURE 2P

FRONT DOOR

STREET

CHARTING THE FLYING STARS IN THE CENTER

Once you have figured out the sitting and facing sides of the space you want to analyze, you can then take the Period Star that you've placed in the sitting palace and place that same Star into the center palace. You are now about to build a Flying Star chart for the whole house.

Let us say you are working with a Period 6 house that sits in the South. If you go back to the Period Star chart, you can see that for the Period 6 House the South palace will have the number 1 (see below). So you place the number 1 in the center palace, *above* the Period Star that has already been placed in the center. The Period Star is also referred to as the Time Star or the Construction Cycle number by other Feng Shui schools. There is a universal way of arranging these Stars, and the Period Star always remains underneath the other two Stars that will be placed in each sector or palace.

SE		S		SW	
	5		1		3
E		**1**		W	
	4		6		8
NE		N		NW	
	9		2		7

V

Referring to the chart above, the 1 Star in the center came from the Period 1 Star in the sitting palace of the South-sitting Period 6 House.

You will also notice that the Period Star in the North palace is 2, so you will end up putting a number 2 in the center also for this house type. Usually, this pairing of numbers will be written with a hyphen (-) in between them (see below).

	S	
		1
	1-2	
		6
	N	
		2

V

The numbers we just added to the center palace, to join the Period Star, are now referred to jointly as the "Center Stars." The number on the left of the hyphen is called the "Mountain Star," and the number on the right side of the hyphen is called the "Water Star." Each sector will end up having a Mountain Star and a Water Star. Later in the book you will be introduced to the Five Elements: Water, Wood, Fire, Earth, and Metal. The expressions "Mountain Star" and "Water Star" are *not* literally associated with elements of Earth or Water, to be discussed in later chapters.

Some schools refer to the Mountain Star as a "people number" or the "sitting number" because mountain/people/sitting relates to health and human harmony. That will always be the emphasis of that number/Star. This will become clear in the next chapter when the definitions of the Stars and how each Star can affect the occupants of a house are outlined.

The Star on the right side of the hyphen is called the Water Star and referred to as well as the "money number" or the "facing number." Water/money/facing relates to the occupants' careers more than their health or relationships, although some number combinations are interchangeable in their meanings or effects on people. Examples of that will be given in the chapter that goes over what the number combinations mean.

And this is how you will begin plotting out each chart you do. You will take the Period Stars from the sitting and facing palaces and bring them into the center palace, paired as Mountain Star and Water Star.

CHARTING THE MOUNTAIN STAR

The number you have placed in the center as the Mountain Star is then going to *ascend or descend* to all the other directions in that same pattern of: center, Northwest, West, Northeast, South, North, Southwest, East, Southeast. The question is: *Do you ascend or descend the numbers?* This is all determined based on the "gender" of the number, coupled with what precise compass alignment the structure has. For example, it is no longer good enough to note which of the eight basic directions a house sits. Each of the eight basic directions has three subdivisions, which are also called sectors, totaling twenty-four different possible directions/sectors a house can sit. Review Fig. 2G.

By knowing whether a house sits in the first sector of a direction or the second and third sectors, you will then know whether you *ascend* the number pattern through all the directions or whether you *descend* the number pattern. At this point I am using the word "sector" to describe one of the three sub-directions of each of the eight major directions.

For example: the direction West has three 15-degree sectors within its 45-degree range. As shown in Fig. 2G, there are West 1, West 2, and West 3.

You now need to memorize the "gender" of the Period Star from the sitting and facing palaces in order to know whether you ascend or descend the number pattern. So, yes, these are new terms and concepts.

The numbers 1, 3, 7, and 9 are "yang" or masculine numbers for the purposes of charting out the Flying Star chart. The odd number 5 will be discussed later in this chapter.

The numbers 2, 4, 6, and 8 are "yin" or feminine numbers for the purposes of charting out the Flying Star chart.

This, by the way, has nothing to do with what you will learn later on about the numbers/Stars as the Trigrams they represent and what family member they represent, which will be discussed in the next chapter. These gender specifications are just for you to know whether you chart out the numbers/Stars in a descending or ascending pattern.

If you have a sitting number that is 1, 3, 7, or 9 and the house sits in the *first sector* of *any direction*, then you will ascend the numbers throughout the rest of the chart.

If the house sits in the *second or third sector* of any direction, then you do the exact opposite, which would be to descend the sequence of numbers if the sitting number is 1, 3, 7, or 9.

Go back to the chart of the house that sits South and note there is a 1 in the sitting palace. If that house sits S1 (first sector of South), then you will *ascend* the numbers throughout the rest of the directions. If that house sits South 2 (S2) or South 3 (S3), however, you would *de-*

scend the numbers because a house that sits in the second or third sectors of any direction indicates that you will do the *exact opposite* of what the number's gender implies. Here are the comparable charts to review.

This first example is for a house that sits South 1. Since it is in the first sector, you treat the Period Star for what it is (1 is yang, which means ascending). Below you will see the Mountain Stars plotted (in bold type) in each sector, ascending from 1 in the center, 2 in Northwest, 3 in West, 4 in Northeast, 5 in South, 6 in North, 7 in Southwest, 8 in East, and 9 in Southeast.

SE 9-
     5
	S 5-
	    1
		SW 7-
		     3

E   8-
    4
	1-2
	6
		W 3-
		    8

NE 4-
     9
	N 6-
	    2
		NW 2-
		    7

V

Now, if this same Period 6 House were sitting South 2 or South 3, you would *descend* the number pattern throughout the chart. See below:

SE 2-
     5
	S 6-
	    1
		SW 4-
		     3

E   3-
    4
	1-2
	6
		W 8-
		    8

NE 7-
     9
	N 5-
	    2
		NW 9-
		    7

V

This comparison of the two Mountain Star charts should underscore how important it is to do an accurate compass reading first and then float your numbers/Stars correctly second. You are going to wind up with a totally different house type if a house sits 165 degrees (South 1) versus 175 degrees (South 2). It is only a 10 degree difference in orientation, but it will be a dramatically different house.

Reminder: You do not automatically ascend or descend the pattern based on the gender of the Period Star in the facing and sitting palaces. *You must also note whether the sitting and facing directions are in the first, second, or third sectors of that direction.* For a house that sits/faces in the second or third sectors of a direction, you will do the *opposite* of either the ascending or descending pattern, based on the "gender" of the number.

CHARTING THE WATER STAR

To map out the facing number (Water Star) throughout the chart, you follow the same principles: Look at the Period Star in the facing palace and/or the Water Star in the center palace (which is the same number that came from the facing palace.)

Determine whether that number is inherently "yin," which implies descending movement. This would be a facing number that is 2, 4, 6, or 8. If the number is 1, 3, 7, or 9, then it is inherently "yang," which implies ascending movement throughout the chart.

But then you must *pay attention* to whether your compass reading yields a first sector facing or a second or third sector facing. You can assume (but should verify with your compass reading) that the facing sector position will mirror whatever the sitting position is. This is assuming that almost all houses have parallel sitting and facing walls. So, if the house sits East 1, then it is most likely facing West 1. If a house sits NW 3, then it will face SE 3 unless the house has non-parallel sitting and facing walls.

If there is ever any discrepancy between the facing wall and the sitting wall's direction, (i.e., they are not parallel), then you need to consider the whole orientation of the structure to be based on the *sitting direction.* For example, if you are reviewing a building that does not have parallel walls and the back wall sits West 1 and the front wall truly faces East 3, then you need to consider the whole structure to be sitting West 1 and *continue to do the chart for a West 1 sitting building (as if it also faced East 1).* This just means that the facing wall is angled about 30 degrees away from being parallel to the back wall, which does happen occasionally on purpose with more unusual architectural designs.

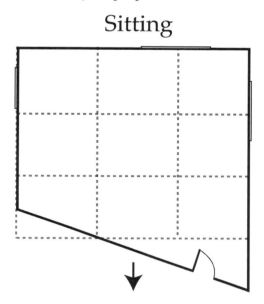

Sitting

To repeat, a facing wall might not be parallel to a sitting wall, but as you make your Flying Star chart for that structure, the calculations will be based *as if* the sitting and facing walls are parallel.

FIGURE 2Q. The floor plan in Fig. 2Q shows that sitting and facing walls are not parallel; however, the chart to be drawn up for it will appear as an overlay, as if the sitting and facing walls were parallel.

The key is to understand that the inherent character of the structure relies on the sitting side, the spine or back of the structure. This is like a person whose spine is aligned in one direction but whose head is turned to face a slightly different direction, not parallel to his or her spine.

Using the same chart example for the Period 6 house that sits South 1 and floating the Water Star numbers as well, you come up with this complete Flying Star chart:

SE 9-3	S 5-7	SW 7-5
5	1	3
E 8-4	1-2	W 3-9
4	6	8
NE 4-8	N 6-6	NW 2-1
9	2	7

V

HOW TO TREAT THE NUMBER 5 STAR IN THE SITTING OR FACING PALACE

In the previous section, it is noted that 1, 3, 7, and 9 are "yang" numbers and 2, 4, 6, and 8 are "yin" numbers. *But what about the number 5?* What happens with the number 5 when it lands in a sitting or facing palace and then becomes one of the Center Stars? How do you determine the ascending or descending status of this chart?

Consider the 5 Star to be a chameleon, not just in this instance but in other Feng Shui formulae that you will learn about. So, the 5 Star will take on the "gender" of whatever the Period Star is.

In other words, if a house was built in Period 2, 4, 6, or 8, then the 5 Star will mimic that energy and be inherently "yin." If the house was built in Period 1, 3, 7, or 9, then the 5 Star will be considered inherently "yang." Here is an example below of a chart for a *SE2 sitting* house, built in Period 6:

E 3-9	SE 4-8	S 9-3
4	**5**	1
NE 8-4	5-7	SW 2-1
9	6	3
N 1-2	NW 6-6	W 7-5
2	7	8

V

Notice the 5 Star in the Sitting Palace. It is the Period Star in the SE sector in bold type. Because the House was built in Period 6, this particular 5 Star in the SE is going to take on "yin" characteristics (with an inherently descending number pattern like all the yin numbers). But you would only carry out that descending pattern if the house were sitting SE1. Since it was arbitrarily decided that this chart would be for an SE2 *sitting* house, you do the opposite of what you would do with a first sector sitting position. Therefore, you will float that sitting number in an *ascending* pattern as shown. The Period number in the facing palace, number 7 (inherently yang), switches to a yin descending pattern because the chart example is for a 2nd sector of NW-facing and not the first sector of NW-facing.

In Chapter Four of this book, all 144 possible charts are printed, which allows you to check your own calculations to make sure you have done your chart correctly.

SUPERIMPOSING THE FLYING STAR CHART OVER THE FLOOR PLAN

Fig. 2R shows an example of a floor plan with a luo shu grid superimposed over it and the complete Flying Star chart for that house type.

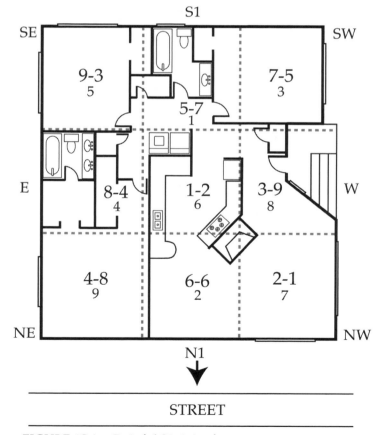

FIGURE 2R is a Period 6 S1 sitting house.

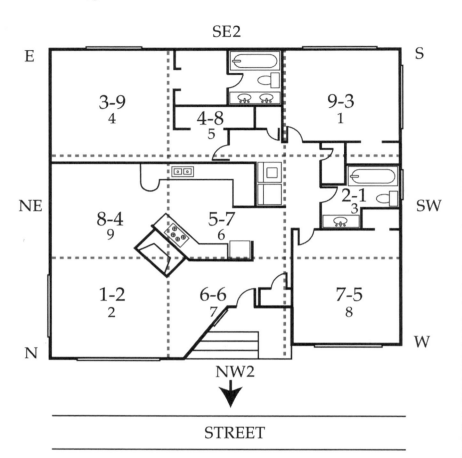

FIGURE 2S is a Period 6 SE2 sitting house.

CHAPTER THREE

Interpreting the Stars and Their Combinations

The numbers are code for energy. And that energy can have a multitude of influences on occupants. Each number (a Flying Star) can represent an element, an image, a direction, a member of the family, a stage in life, a major time frame, or parts of the body. A serious student of Feng Shui will need to memorize all these attributes of each Flying Star. It all seems very academic and dry initially, but as soon as you have an experience with the Flying Stars, you will remember their meanings easily. Additionally, the Stars go through good and bad cycles, which stretch over a 180-year Cycle, and the Star combinations can represent certain circumstances or events, which will be covered in a separate section. This 180-year Cycle that each Star goes through is broken down into three major sixty-year Periods. Like spokes on a wheel that turns perpetually, when a Star begins a Period that is forty years away from matching its own Star Period, it begins a good "Sheng" phase that gets better and better until the twenty-year era when it reigns as the "Wang" number (i.e., strongest, the best). Then, when its twenty-year reign is over, the Star begins long declining cycles referred to as "death and decay." These Periods are also referred to as "untimely."

Below is a chart that shows the last complete cycle of the three major sixty-year Cycles, which are each broken down into twenty-year Periods. The major sixty-year Cycles are called "Yuans."

Yuan	Yun-Period	20-Year Era
Upper	1	1864–1883
	2	1884–1903
	3	1904–1923
Middle	4	1924–1943
	5	1944–1963
	6	1964–1983
Lower	7	1984–2003
	8	2004–2023
	9	2024–2043

This 180-year Cycle will continue with the next Upper Yuan Cycle, beginning with the next Period 1 starting in 2044. Stars are considered untimely when they are not in their Sheng or Wang phase. Some Stars are inherently good, and even when they are untimely, you can still get some positive effects of them. The Stars that are inherently good are 1, 6, 8, and 9. The Stars that are inherently bad are 2, 3, 4, 5, and 7. So when they are not in a Sheng or Wang phase, more of their negative attributes become manifest. I personally think the 4 Star can swing either way and have a positive influence even when it is not "timely." The 9 Star is known for "intensifying" the timely and untimely Stars in any Period.

THE INDIVIDUAL FLYING STARS
1 THROUGH 9

Flying Star Number 1
- Trigram Name: Kan (the "a" is like "ah")
- Element: water
- Color: blue or black
- Image: Deep body of water like the bottom of the ocean or a swift-moving river. The image of water can also lend itself to water-related circumstances or businesses, such as the fishing or shipping industry.
- Inherent Direction: North
- Family Member: middle son or a middle-aged man
- Parts of the Body: kidneys, blood, circulation, ears, bladder
- Major Construction Era Associated with the Number: Period 1
- Impact of the 1 Star When It Is in a *Good/Great Phase*: power and affluence, wisdom and spirituality
- Impact When the 1 Star Is in a *Negative Phase*: impotence and problems related to the Kan body areas.

Flying Star Number 2
- Trigram Name: Kun (sounds like "tune" with a "k")
- Element: soft earth
- Color: shades of orange, yellow, or brown
- Image: Soil, sand, the earth, and a vast piece of land. The image of land could also affect or be applicable to farming, geology, or archeology. An example might be a farmer who has a permanent 2 Star at his front door. People are often attracted to certain Flying Stars that accentuate who they are or what they do for a living.
- Inherent Direction: Southwest
- Family Member: mother or a nurturer
- Parts of the Body: abdominal area, including digestion, elimination, reproductive organs

- Major Construction Era Associated with the Number: Period 2
- Impact of the 2 Star When It Is in a *Good/Great Phase*: fertility, female leadership, owner of land, real estate
- Impact When the 2 Star Is in a *Negative Phase*: sickness, loneliness, depression, bleeding, miscarriage, or problems related to the Kun body areas

Flying Star Number 3

- Trigram Name: Zhen (rhymes with "pen," starts with a "ch" sound)
- Element: hard wood
- Color: all shades of green
- Image: Thunder. This image can be literal or figurative, such as a loud booming noise.
- Inherent Direction: East
- Family Member: eldest son, also symbolic of a prince or vice-president, second in command
- Parts of the Body: feet, throat, nervous system, including convulsions or hysteria. Stuttering also appears to be a Zhen-related problem.
- Major Construction Era Associated with the Number: Period 3
- Impact of the 3 Star When It Is in a *Good /Great Phase*: wealth, leadership, the man who can be master of "pen and sword"
- Impact When the 3 Star Is in a *Negative Phase*: arguments, gossip, theft, legal issues, or problems related to the Zhen body areas

Flying Star Number 4

- Trigram Name: Xun (sounds like "shoon")
- Element: soft wood
- Color: all shades of green
- Inherent Direction: Southeast
- Image: The Wind, a Traveler. This image signifies movement and a spirit of adventure. It would be very much in character for a travel agency to have a permanent 4 Star at its entry door.

- Family Member: eldest daughter
- Parts of the Body: low back, hips, buttocks, thighs, knees
- Major Construction Era Associated with the Number: Period 4
- Impact of the 4 Star When It Is in a *Good/Great Phase*: supportive of creative endeavors, art, music, writing, acting, academia, and romance
- Impact When the 4 Star Is in a *Negative Phase*: romantic heartbreak, infidelity, or sexual scandal and manipulation

Flying Star Number 5

- Trigram Name: none, although the 5 Star is sometimes called the "Emperor"
- Element: earth
- Color: shades of yellow, orange, or brown
- Image: none
- Inherent Direction: Center
- Inherent Family Member: none
- Parts of the Body: There are no specific body areas like the other Trigrams, although some believe the 5 Star can influence cells and skin.
- Major Construction Era Associated with the Number: Period 5
- Impact of the 5 Star When It Is in a *Good/Great Phase*: major prosperity star, wealth and fame
- Impact When the 5 Star Is in a *Negative Phase*: arguments, accidents, delays, pain, diseases, disaster, ignorance, procrastination, or laziness. This is the Star most related to cancer.

Flying Star Number 6

- Trigram Name: Qian (pronounced "chee-yen")
- Element: hard metal
- Color: gold, silver, gray, or white
- Image: Heaven. The image of Heaven also implies anything that is higher in comparison to something lower. For example, a room can

be divided into three levels, with the top third of a room up to the ceiling being referred to as the "heaven" level, the middle third being the level of man, and the lower third of the room being referred to as the "earth" level.

- Inherent Direction: Northwest
- Inherent Family Member: father, also any male authority figure
- Parts of the Body: head, lungs
- Major Construction Era Associated with the Number: Period 6
- Impact of the 6 Star When It Is in a *Good/Great Phase*: power and authority, advances in technology and science, ambition and responsibility
- Impact When the 6 Star Is in a *Negative Phase*: isolation, loneliness, problems with the government, diseases related to the head or lungs

Flying Star Number 7

- Trigram Name: Dui (pronounced "dway")
- Element: soft metal
- Color: gold, silver, gray, or white
- Image: A shallow lake like a marsh, laughing girls. These two images do not seem connected; but with deeper study and understanding of the Trigrams and the Yi Jing, we discover that the Trigrams are profound and have even more meanings than are listed here. An all-girls school with the 7 Star prominent at the front doors is just an example of how the Feng Shui can match the function of a space.
- Inherent Direction: West
- Inherent Family Member: youngest daughter
- Parts of the Body: teeth, whole mouth area, jaw, breasts
- Major Construction Era Associated with the Number: Period 7
- Impact of the 7 Star When It Is in a *Good/Great phase*: competitive success, prosperity, verbal skills and communication, divination
- Impact When the 7 Star Is in a *Negative Phase*: cheating, betrayal, deception, embezzlement, assault, fire, sex-related diseases, or injury

The last Period 7 created major sources of communication, including cell phones and the Internet. The 7 Star's association with divination and with young women also explains why Feng Shui became so popular worldwide in Period 7. Young women fueled the interest in Feng Shui worldwide.

Flying Star Number 8

- Trigram Name: Gen (pronounced like "gun")
- Element: hard earth
- Color: shades of brown, yellow, or orange
- Image: Mischievous child, a monk on a hill. Here, again, we have seemingly contradictory images. When more data is corroborated with a Flying Star, then it becomes more apparent how it will manifest or whom it will affect. Usually the 8 Star is associated with children and boys in particular. But the image of a monk could also manifest as a man who is celibate by choice or circumstance.
- Inherent Direction: Northeast
- Inherent Family Member: youngest son
- Parts of the Body: bones, muscles, joints, and the spine
- Major Construction Era Associated with the Number: Period 8
- Impact of the 8 Star When It Is in a *Good/Great Phase*: prosperity, happiness, celebrations, family harmony, and success of young people
- Impact When the 8 Star Is in a *Negative Phase*: scoliosis or other problems related to the Gen body areas, along with injuries to children, bad luck

Flying Star Number 9

- Trigram Name: Li (pronounced "lee")
- Element: fire
- Color: hot shades of red, maroon, burgundy, cranberry
- Image: Fire. This image can be one of purification, but fire is symbolic of explosions, electrical problems, or lightning.

- Inherent Direction: South
- Inherent Family Member: middle daughter or a middle-aged woman
- Parts of the Body: eyes, heart
- Major Construction Era Associated with the Number: Period 9
- Impact of the 9 Star When It Is in a *Good/Great Phase*: prosperity, success, and achievement
- Impact When the 9 Star Is in a *Negative Phase*: insanity, fire accidents or explosions, heart and eye diseases

These Stars/Trigrams are loaded with meaning, and there are many mystical ways of looking at them individually as well as in certain arrangements. There is a "Pre-Heaven" Sequence in which the Trigrams are arranged as below. Some Feng Shui calculations and insights are gleaned from this Pre-Heaven arrangement, which is symbolic of life before we incarnate on planet Earth. Notice that the Trigrams are paired as follows:

- Mother-Father Trigrams are placed opposite each other.
- Eldest Son and Eldest Daughter are poised to be opposite each other.
- Middle Son and Middle Daughter are opposite.
- Youngest Son and Youngest Daughter are opposite.

Pre-Heaven Sequence

SE	S	SW
DUI	QIAN	XUN
LI (E)		KAN (W)
ZHEN	KUN	GEN
NE	N	NW

FIGURE 3A is an illustration of the Pre-Heaven chart, showing the arrangements of the Trigrams in each direction.

Some of the terms and concepts relating to the Flying Stars really do need more in-depth explanations and references about how they came about than what I provide here. My focus has always been to work with the Flying Stars as a practitioner, more than an academic, and I don't want to bog down the instructional emphasis of this book with too many historical references. For more detailed information about such things as the Pre-Heaven Sequence and the relationship between the Flying Stars and aspects of actual astronomy, I can recommend Stephen Skinner's book called *Flying Star Feng Shui*. His book has a unique angle, and he also lists in his references a few books that were written by some former students of Master Sang.

Most Feng Shui calculations are based on an arrangement called the "Later Heaven or Post-Heaven Sequence," shown in Fig. 3B. Here the Trigrams are assigned directions, which will be emphasized in the analysis of houses and buildings. The Trigrams in this arrangement are used most of the time, for example, with the Northwest being associated with the Qian Trigram and all the symbolism it contains.

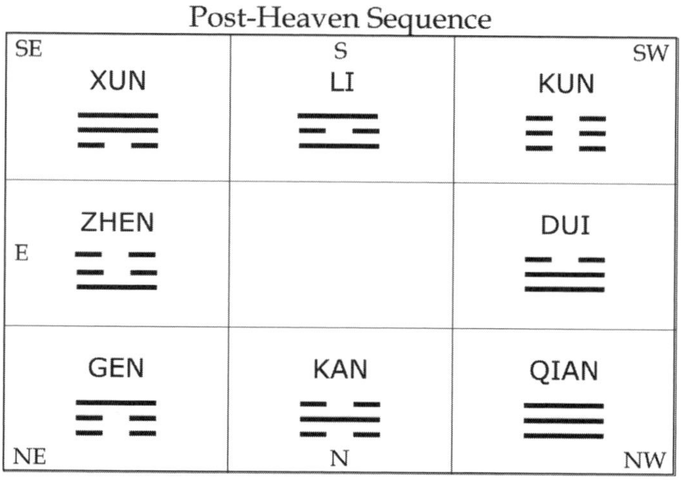

Post-Heaven Sequence

SE XUN	S LI	SW KUN
E ZHEN		DUI
NE GEN	N KAN	NW QIAN

FIGURE 3B

CHART COMBINING THE PRE-HEAVEN AND POST-HEAVEN TRIGRAM ARRANGEMENTS

In the chart below "PR" stands for *Pre-Heaven* and "PO" stands for *Post-Heaven*. Comparing this overlay and relationship, the combined chart helps explain why certain Stars are considered "usable" in a particular Period, even if those Stars are in an "untimely" phase. This will be referenced again later in the book.

SE PR: Dui PO: Xun	S PR: Qian PO: Li	SW PR: Xun PO: Kun
E PR: Li PO: Zhen	CENTER There is no Trigram associated with center	W PR: Kan PO: Dui
NE PR: Zhen PO: Gen	N PR: Kun PO: Kan	NW PR: Gen PO: Qian

Looking at the combined chart, you can locate the ruling Star for any given Period and see which untimely Stars might actually be less negative during that timeframe because they are paired up with them. For example: If you locate the placement of Dui, you will see that it appears in the Southeast as a Pre-Heaven location and is joined by the Xun Star. Dui also appears in the West as a Post-Heaven location, paired up with the Kan Star as a Pre-Heaven location. So, during Period 7 (Dui), the supposedly "untimely" nature of the 1 (Kan) and 4 (Xun) Stars were considered more usable.

An important note: Some of you reading this book already know there is a Trigram related to your year of birth and gender. In *The Feng Shui Matrix*, I cover a lot of information related to your Personal Trigram.

But it should be understood that even though some negative connotations are associated with these Trigrams (as Flying Stars), that is in no way an indication of or a reflection on your personality or values. For example, in Period 8, the 3 Star in someone's house can make someone argumentative or gossipy. It *does not* mean that Zhen people (Personal Trigram 3) are more argumentative or gossipy than anyone else. So, in other words, *don't* take the definitions of the Trigrams described for a space or time as character traits for people who share the same Trigram as a Personal Trigram.

ADDITIONAL SYMBOLISM ASSOCIATED WITH THE FLYING STARS

Each Flying Star is associated with other characteristics, and those characteristics have both enduring features as well as changing features. In the individual Flying Star List that begins this chapter, each Flying Star is in its best phase during the Construction Period associated with it. For example, during Period 5, the 5 Star is extremely positive and considered a prosperity Star. But in Period 8, the 5 Star has mostly negative characteristics that will influence a building's occupants.

As mentioned earlier, each Flying Star progresses through a 180-year-Cycle. Below is a chart showing the phases that each Star goes through. Like life for human beings, we start out in a positive phase where we grow, get stronger, and reach maturity. But then there is a long downward cycle until we die. And for those of you who believe in reincarnation, we are re-born to start the cycle over again. These Flying Stars "live" their life, get worn out, get sick (metaphorically speaking), and then die. But they are reborn every 180 years.

180-YEAR CYCLE OF THE STARS

For the chart below: "P" stands for Period. P8 means "Period 8."

Star Impact	Sheng Phase During	Wang Phase During	Shuai Phase During	Si Phase During
1	P8, P9	P1	P2, P3	P4,5,6,7
2	P9, P1	P2	P3, P4	P5,6,7,8
3	P1, 2	P3	P4, P5	P6,7,8,9
4	P2, P3	P4	P5, P6	P7,8,9,1
5	P3, P4	P5	P6, P7	P8,9,1,2
6	P4, P5	P6	P7, P8	P9,1,2,3
7	P5, P6	P7	P8, P9	P1,2,3,4
8	P6, P7	P8	P9, P1	P2,3,4,5
9	P7, P8	P9	P1, P2	P3,4,5,6

This discussion refers to the chart in column one. The 8 Star is in a Sheng cycle in P6 and P7. Across the columns, the 8 Star is in a Wang Phase in P8. Then the drop off or decline begins in P9. Sheng translates as "life," and it implies life encouraging or nurturing. When a Star is in the Sheng Phase, it has a positive influence in that Period that could be called very good. Wang implies strong and greatest prosperity. This is the excellent energy for twenty years. The Shuai cycle is a state of decaying, and the Si cycle is a death phase. Each Star is in these two last cycles for a combined 120 years.

The chart above explains why a house might have a good influence on its occupants for decades and then turn a corner where it will not be good for a long time or vice versa.

As an example, in Period 8, the 8 Star is quite positive and indicates great prosperity and health. But in Period 2 you can see that the 8 Star was in a very bad phase.

Let us say that the 8 Star lands in someone's bedroom. The bedroom is used as an example because it is the room that virtually everyone spends the most time in. During the Great Phase of the 8 Star, the 8 would indicate the occupant could be well off financially. But in Period 2, when the 8 Star is negative, it could indicate that the occupants could have severe bone or muscle problems (like scoliosis). This is because the 8 Star is always related to the bones and muscles. You can always refer to the parts of the body that a Trigram/Star represents. When that Star is in a bad phase, it is going to reveal a particular harshness to that area of the body associated with the Trigram.

I also want to emphasize here that I am only interpreting how the Flying Stars might behave in any house, built in any Period. It does not mean the *entire* house is bad once it has outlived its original Construction Period. In other words, a house built in Period 5 is not necessarily a bad house in Period 8. It just means that the effects of the Flying Stars *within* specific locations in that house have changed their influence. In fact, there are even house types that get better in a Period after the one in which they were built. This is based entirely on the floor plan and where the Wang and Sheng Flying Stars for that Period reside. There are a couple of well-known authors who have given readers the erroneous impression that they should only live in a house that was built in the current Period or, if they cannot afford to move into one, that they have to do all kinds of remodel tricks to turn their house into a Current Era House. *This is absolutely not true.*

Some schools of Feng Shui teach that an untimely Star can be in a neutral phase sometime while it is cycling through the 180-year span, and this was the point of showing the Pre-Heaven and Post-Heaven charts combined. Without getting into the deeper meanings, it just very basically shows how you figure out the relationships of the Stars.

Students have gotten the impression that you do not need to remedy a Star in a neutral or "usable" phase, but if it is joined with another Star to create a domination relationship, then I still think it is important to do the elemental remedy, be it reductive or controlling. This will be explained later in the chapter. If you refer back to the chart that combines the Pre-Heaven arrangement with the Post-Heaven arrangement, you can see a specific pairing of Stars that will benefit each other.

Look again to the combined chart and see what the 8 (Gen) Star is paired with: It is paired with 3 in the Northeast and 6 in the Northwest. Some schools teach that this means the 3 and 6 Stars are "usable" in Period 8. This would mean that they are not as bad in their influence in Period 8 as they were in Period 7. There is a "reprieve" from their negative influence even though they are in a long-term "untimely" phase. I did thousands of readings during Period 7, and I was in fact amazed at how positive the 4 Star was in its influence on people, even though it is not anywhere near its next sheng cycle. This supports the theory of the 4 Star being "usable" during Period 7.

In Period 9, the combined chart indicates that the 6 Star and the 3 Star will again be "usable" even as they are "untimely" in Period 9. This does not mean these Stars are positive. But some schools consider these stars "weak" or worn out and not able to do as much harm as they would in other untimely phases.

THE FIVE ELEMENTS AND THEIR THREE CYCLES OF RELATIONSHIP

After reviewing the Flying Stars and their meanings, you must understand that these Stars do not really exist singularly. They are always combined with another Star, and it is the combination of the Stars (as elements) that can reveal how these Flying Stars will behave. Inherent in the combinations is also a solution to potential problems as well as a way to make good combinations even better. In order to do this and to use the proper element as a remedy, you need to learn more about the elements and their relationships with each other.

Examples of What the Elements Are

The Five Elements can be described in various ways, as they are both literal and symbolic. Five-Element theory is used in other systems of Chinese Metaphysics, such as Chinese astrology, but also in Chinese medicine. When one element is out of balance with another, it can reveal a certain health problem. So, too, in your home, if an element is out of balance with another, it can reveal a health problem and much more.

Sometimes these Five Elements are called Five Phases as one blends into the other. The Five Elements can also be linked with the seasons of the year.

Element	Season
Water	Winter
Wood	Spring
Fire	Summer
Earth	Late Summer
Metal	Autumn

First, let's review what the elements are more literally and how to manifest them in a real design or décor format. We have five elements: Water, Wood, Fire, Earth, and Metal.

Water is literally water. Clean, circulating water can change the energy of a room. For an ordinary-sized room, a common indoor fountain that holds a few quarts to a few gallons of water should make a difference. Aquariums can also work as they hold a large amount of water in a small space. But the lid covering of an aquarium must be partially open so that the water can touch the air in the room. In other words, an aquarium will not work if it is totally sealed up. One Feng Shui practitioner local to my area instructs clients to place sealed-up water bottles inside of closets, but this is not the correct usage of water. And fish are just an excuse to move the water around. So it is really just a myth that having fish is somehow a remedy by itself. Water that circulates is usually more effective than just a bowl of water. Very large displays of blue and black, such as an entire wall painted these colors, can be a weak substitute for water. One time I had a job evaluating a tire shop. In theory, it needed water right in the area where the cars would enter and be hoisted up for a tire change. The owners obviously could not put a fountain in this area, but they did the next best thing by painting the concrete floor black to emulate some of the water vibration needed for that area.

Wood is literally a live plant with green, bushy leaves. A plant must be lush and healthy to work as a wood remedy. Dead or dying plants drag energy down. Fake plants do not do anything when you need the wood element. In fact, wood floors and wood furniture are pretty neutral as far as elements go. A very large display of green color, such as a green carpet or a green wall, can be a weak manifestation of the wood element. Some people choose to use the real element as well as back-up reinforcement with the complementary color.

Fire is literally a fire burning. But this is harder to manifest safely in most rooms in a house. Generally, I do not recommend you burn candles for this reason. Of course, supervised candle burning is acceptable. But a significant display of red color can work well. Red color includes shades darker than primary red, such as maroon or burgundy. Depending on the room where fire is needed, you can use drapery, rugs, mats, artwork, or even a piece of furniture that is painted red or has red fabric. An alternative to using a red-colored object is accent lighting, which can produce some heat for at least a few hours per day or night in the area designated for fire.

Earth is anything made of stone, soil, clay, brick, ceramic, concrete, or other earthen materials, including natural gemstones. Usually many pounds of earth are necessary to change the qi (energy) of a room. It is true that a potted plant can be a combination of wood and earth, and you will learn about circumstances where it is okay to have both wood and earth together. Sometimes earth occurs naturally in a room. Let us say your living room happens to need earth and you see that your fireplace façade is stone. That works! Earth colors include any shades of brown, orange, or yellow.

Metal is anything made out of gold, silver, brass, bronze, copper, iron, or steel. Some Chinese folk remedies, like statuary that is made of metal or Chinese gold coins or brass Mandarin ducks, all come from the need to represent metal. In modern times it is very easy to represent metal because so much of our furniture and décor items are made of metal materials, from wrought-iron table legs, steel file cabinets, lamp bases, picture frames, to even appliances such as washer/dryers and refrigerators. Metal colors, such as white, silver, gold, and gray, are a weak substitute for real metal.

The Flying Star charts, superimposed over a floor plan, reveal that seemingly empty rooms and spaces contain a combination of elements in the very qi of the room. Then, actually adding real elements to the room (via color and décor items) will either activate or suppress those inherent forces.

All five elements, listed below for handy reference, have shapes associated with them. But the shapes of small objects of décor are not going to be a satisfactory replacement for a real element. For example, if a room needs the metal element as a cure, using an object that is round in shape will not completely fix the problem. You usually need many pounds of metal to work.

Element	Shape
Water	Wavy
Wood	Column-like
Fire	Pyramid
Earth	Square
Metal	Round

PRIORITY OF THE MOUNTAIN AND WATER STARS

In each section of the house, there are three Numbers/Stars generated: the Construction Cycle Number (aka the Time Star or Period Star), the sitting number (aka Mountain Star), and the facing number (aka Water Star.) Most of the time you will be comparing the Mountain Star with the Water Star, and the Period Star will only have a shadow influence. The Period Star has much less influence, but there will be circumstances in which you will, in fact, look at all three Stars. Generally speaking, when you see a pairing of numbers with a hyphen (-) in between them, it is a reference for the Mountain Star and the Water Star. As an example, 6-8 means "6 Mountain Star and 8 Water Star."

In the following sections you will see combinations of Stars that represent the various elements. Sometimes the elements will be in conflict with each other (a domination cycle), and sometimes you will like the meaning of one Star but not the other. These instances of "mixed messages" are very common. When you know what the Star means (and the element it represents), you can decide whether you want to stimulate it with a productive element or suppress it/weaken it with a reductive element. When you understand the relationship of the Stars with each other, you will know which Star will be most affected.

PRODUCTIVE CYCLE OF THE ELEMENTS

When one element strengthens or "produces" another element, you are going to bring out the qualities (for good or for bad) of the strengthened element. This is why you need to be familiar with the *meanings* of the Stars and not just which element they represent.

- Water strengthens (nurtures) Wood
- Wood strengthens (creates) Fire
- Fire strengthens (turns into) Earth
- Earth strengthens (produces) Metal
- Metal strengthens (becomes like) Water

If you discover that you like the meaning of a certain Star and want to make it more active and influential in a room, then you would use the productive cycle. You would add to the room the element that nurtures the Star you want to activate.

For example, the 4 Star still has many positive connotations, even though it is in a bad phase in Period 8. The 4 Star is the Xun Trigram (Wood), so the way you can strengthen it is by adding water to the area where the 4 Star resides.

Destructive Cycle of the Elements
- Water destroys (puts out) Fire
- Fire destroys (melts) Metal
- Metal destroys (chops) Wood
- Wood destroys (depletes) Earth
- Earth destroys (absorbs) Water

If you do not like the meaning of a particular Star, you could choose to add an element that would "destroy it." This will be done with some Star combinations when *both stars* are negative as well. You will see that the suggested element to cure the whole combination will often dominate one Star and reduce the other Star. It is a way of canceling out the whole energy pattern. But you need to be careful when using a dominating element to cure a problem. It is often better to use the Reductive Cycle (to be explained later) when possible. To use an analogy: You could decide to blow up a time bomb in a controlled setting, and things might work out okay. But it is usually better to *diffuse* the bomb instead. It is the Reductive Cycle element that can siphon off or drain the dominating element in a pairing of Stars. It is the safer way, like diffusing the bomb instead of blowing it up.

Reductive Cycle of the Elements
- Water reduces Metal
- Metal reduces Earth
- Earth reduces Fire
- Fire reduces Wood
- Wood reduces Water

The 5 Star is going to have negative influences until the next Period 3, when the 5 Star will enter a nicer phase (sheng), leading up to its next Wang cycle in the next Period 5. This means that 95% of the time you will want to weaken the 5 Star until it enters that good phase, wherever it lands in your home for many more decades. (This book has been written in Period 8.)

Referring to the Reductive Cycle, Metal reduces Earth. Since the 5 Star is inherently Earth, you can add a lot of metal objects to a room with the 5 Star in it, and that will take away or nullify its power completely. You don't have to be worried about adding too much metal as a remedy most of the time. Many pounds, even fifty to a hundred pounds, are not too much for an ordinary-sized room.

In the Domination Cycle you can see that Wood destroys Earth. You might wonder, "Why can't I just use Wood to destroy the 5 Earth Star?" Let us just say that it is a more aggressive approach (blowing up the bomb), and there could be side effects in doing so. It is better to use the Reductive Cycle whenever possible, as that is more gentle and is really just a different way of using the Productive Cycle. For this I also like to use an analogy from martial arts. If a bad guy is lunging toward you to hurt you, you can definitely position yourself to fight back. But in all martial arts schools, you will be taught to a) see if you can just step out of the aggressor's way and let his momentum carry him right past you or b) find a way to cancel out his force without having to use equal or greater force. This includes a lot of techniques where a smaller person can actually learn how to "take down" a bigger, stronger person. Using the Reductive Element is a way of side-stepping or diffusing the dominating element instead of confronting it head-on.

Dominating Element	Tries to Destroy	Reductive Element Is
Water	Fire	Wood
Wood	Earth	Fire
Fire	Metal	Earth
Earth	Water	Metal
Metal	Wood	Water

The Reductive Element mitigates the Controlling Cycle in each example. When Water tries to destroy Fire, Wood is introduced because Water naturally wants to strengthen Wood, and then Wood in turn strengthens Fire. The Reductive Element becomes productive in this sense.

The definitions of these Star combinations to follow are based on the current Period 8 Cycle that this book was written in. These definitions will be mostly accurate in Period 9 as well. Therefore, you have a description of the Flying Star Combinations that will be good until the year 2044. But if you desire to study a structure from decades past or further into the future, you can refer to the definitions given for all the Stars in both their positive and negative phases. You can figure out pretty easily how the influences change over long periods of time. For instance, directly below you will see that the first Star combination, 1-3, has mostly negative connotations, but in less than forty years from now, the 3 Star will be sheng (good) again.

PRODUCTIVE STAR COMBINATIONS

1-3 = 1 Water strengthens 3 Wood. Since the 3 Star now affects most people negatively, you will usually want to *weaken* the 3 Wood Star with Fire. Sometimes you can see that public figures and celebrities personify the 3 Star, both benefiting from and suffering from gossip and legal problems. Someone who deals with contracts and legal matters regularly might be the exception to the rule. If you are a lawyer and your office is in a 1-3 area, then you would not necessarily want to weaken the 3 Star.

1-4 = 1 Water strengthens 4 Wood. Even though the 4 Star is in a bad phase right now, it still represents academia and the arts. It can still help support creative people and creative professions. It can also help people in industries that relate to health and beauty. But the 4 Star is very sexual when it is in a bad phase, and it is no coincidence that our various forms of entertainment, art, and music are very erotic these days. This 4 Star energy can be further strengthened with Water or reduced with Fire.

1-6 = 1 Water is strengthened by 6 Metal. Currently, the 6 Star is in a downward cycle, but it is considered inherently a "good" Star. The combination of 1 and 6 can mean the occupant will be powerful and affluent. No remedies are needed. This is a combination that only needs remedies when a certain annual influence joins it to create an irritation. As an example, if an Annual 2 Star were to join this combination, then only would you need to add Metal, just to cancel out the 2 Star. More information on Annual Stars will be provided in later chapters.

1-7 = 1 Water is strengthened by 7 Metal. The influence of this combination varies. Some definitions include: the occupants will like to entertain a lot, have parties, and possibly drink a lot of alcohol. The 1 Water is symbolic here of alcohol, but this combination can feed other addictive behaviors, including smoking and taking drugs. The 7 (Dui) Star in this combination can also mean the woman will look younger than she is. This is partly due to Dui representing a young pretty girl as a Trigram. In some house types the 1-7 combination comes up twice, and it often matches a male or female occupant who has a lot of clothes and is highly focused on his or her appearance.

2-6 = 2 Earth strengthening 6 Metal. Beginning students often wonder why this productive cycle needs to be remedied. But until the 2 Star moves into a good phase (in 2024), it needs to be reduced with Metal. The 2 sickness Star can trigger health problems related to the head or lungs when it is paired up with 6 Metal. A person could also end up feeling lonely or aloof in the 2-6 energy. And in all these recommendations for elements, you will want to be just as careful to *remove* a harmful element from a room as to add a corrective element. By memorizing the destructive cycle, you will know that fire would be very bad with combinations you are trying to weaken with metal. Metal and fire are a clash. I once went to a client's home who had the 2-6 Flying Stars in her bedroom with a burgundy bedspread. She was very sad because her boyfriend had called off their engagement. I told her to put a lot of metal in her bedroom *and* to remove the red bedspread. Almost immediately her relationship with her boyfriend improved, and she called to say the engagement was back on a couple weeks later.

2-7 = 2 Earth strengthening 7 Metal. Just like the 2-6 combination, you want to suppress the 2 Earth Star with Metal. The 2 Star can trigger sickness or problems related to the mouth, teeth, jaw, or chest area when paired with the 7 Star. The 2 Star can also represent bleeding, and the 7 Star can represent assault or injury, so this combination could predict some violent act.

2-9 = 2 Earth strengthened by 9 Fire. This combination will turn positive in 2024. But, for now, the 2 Star needs to be suppressed with Metal. Otherwise, the negative attributes of the 2 Star will come out. As well, this specific combination can mean a baby may have mental deficiencies like Down's syndrome. It is not good to conceive a baby in a 2-9 section. The 2-9 combination is sometimes found in the rooms of children or teenagers who play with matches or start fires.

3-1 = 3 Wood is strengthened by 1 Water. The meaning is very similar to the 1-3 combination. This is an example where the positioning of the numbers as Mountain Star and Water Star do not make a big difference. One might only guess that, if we relate to the Mountain Star (for people) and the Water Star (for money), the 3-1 and 1-3 combinations might differ in terms of *who* is doing the gossiping? And *who* is creating the legal problems? *Who* is doing the stealing? My guess is that, if you are sleeping in the 1-3 combination, you might be the *perpetrator* of these problems whereas, if you are sleeping in the 3-1 arrangement, you could be the *victim* of these problems. I have seen this combination be almost identical, but if you pay attention to the Mountain Star, notice whether it is receiving energy from the Water Star or vice versa. This can help distinguish the subtlety of whether things are happening to you (outside forces coming to you) or whether you are causing things to happen to others (outside your home, for example). In a legal sense, this might predict whether you are the plaintiff or the defendant! Master Sang has taught a class about how to win a lawsuit, and it gets very specific with the Flying Stars to the point of predicting whether you can a) win a case and win money, b) win a case but lose money, or c) lose a case and lose money or your reputation.

3-9 = 3 Wood strengthening 9 Fire. Most of the time you need to weaken this combination with Fire remedies since the 3 Star in many combinations can imply arguments, gossip, legal woes, or theft. The 9 Star can signify intelligence when it is in a good phase, but insanity when it is in a bad phase. When I first started studying Feng Shui, I was living in a house with a 9 Star at the entrance. The previous occupant lived there during Period 6, when the 9 Star was in a bad phase. I moved into that house later in Period 7 when the 9 Star entered the sheng cycle. I was informed by the neighbors next door that the previous occupant was a mathematician who went berserk when his wife left him. (In this case the 9 Star was paired with a 4 Star, which makes sense for all the symbolism of the 4 Star too.) They used to hear him talking to himself, and he totally neglected the house, letting the grass and weeds grow over six feet tall on the front lawn. My neighbors said that he eventually got better, remarried, and seemed happy again, and all that coincided with the beginning of Period 7 in 1984 when the 9 Star entered the good/sheng phase. So, with the 9 Star being related to intelligence, the 3-9 combination can mean that the boy in that 3-9 bedroom will be smart (but rebellious). The 3 Star can mean that anyone using the room could be argumentative or get embroiled in legal issues. Unless you are an attorney and thrive on legal issues, then it is usually recommended that you weaken this 3 Wood Star with Fire.

4-1 = 4 Wood being strengthened by 1 Water Star. Since the 1 Star is in the "money" position, it is more yang in nature and does the nurturing of the 4 Wood from the outside (such as from people outside the house toward the people inside). This energy can attract love from the outside of the house to the inside. So it is easy for the woman in the house to have boyfriends. It is almost identical to the 1-4 combination, however. This energy often does not need any strengthening, but if you did want to activate it, you could add Water. If the sexual energy was being activated in an inappropriate way, then you would want to reduce it with Fire. The Fire weakens the 4 Wood. You could also "block" the Water with Earth. Having both Earth and Fire together could be an effective way to stop your spouse from cheating on you if you sleep in the 4-1 or 1-4 energy.

Master Sang told a story many years ago about a client of his who confided that his wife was cheating on him. Among the various observations that Master Sang made, he noticed that the couple had a large cracked boulder in their landscape. Master Sang told the man to make sure the cracked boulder was replaced with one that had no crack in it. The man followed his recommendations, and the wife started behaving herself. Years passed, and the problem came up again. Master Sang revisited the man's home to find another cracked boulder in the landscape. So, again he told the man to replace it with a stone without any cracks. This is an example of how Earth can be used to dominate Water in a helpful way. The Earth in this case can block the Water from further stimulating the 4 Wood Star. (Most of the element remedies suggested in this book are for interiors. Sometimes, however, large elements outside a house can influence the Stars inside. For example, a pool very close to a house can affect the Stars inside. Another example could be a bed of red flowers right next to the side of a house, exerting the influence of Fire.) The boulder in Master Sang's case study needed to be in good shape, not cracked, to correct the problem.

Having anything cracked, be it a window, a mirror, or a piece of pottery can also have specific negative affects on the occupants based on the location of the cracked item in combination with the occupant's Chinese Zodiac sign. With enough data, the prediction can be very specific. To avoid these problems altogether, do not let things exist for very long in a broken, cracked, or dilapidated state.

4-9 = 4 Wood strengthening 9 Fire. This combination can indicate the occupant will be artistic or academic or both. But, again, we have to pay attention to who is living in this area with the 4-9 combination. Because the 4 Star is so sexual now, this could also indicate some betrayal or heartbreak in the romance department. The 4 Star is referred to as the "Peach Blossom" Star, which can imply scandalous sexual activity as much as it can innocent romance. To transmute the sexual energy and turn it into more intellectual or spiritual energy, you add Fire. This 4-9 combination will always be tempered by what kind of annual influence is in that area. Sometimes you will want to add Fire, and sometimes you will want to add Water in order to correct some "mini-domination cycles" when yearly forces are added to the mix. It is also entirely possible that the 4 Star will behave differently in creative communities. Having so many clients in the arts and entertainment professions, I see this 4 Star helping the careers of actors, artists, musicians, and writers.

5-6 = 5 Earth strengthening 6 Metal. The 5 Star is going to irritate whatever it is paired with, so you will need to be concerned about the 6 Star here. Inherently one of the "good" Stars, the 6 Star can suggest power and authority being challenged by the 5 Star. The 6 Star is related to the head and lungs, so the 5 Star could bring accident or illness to the head or lungs, including asthma or migraines. It could also irritate or bring misfortune to the father in the house or the president of the company because the 6 Qian Star represents the man in charge. Adding Metal to weaken the 5 Earth Star is the cure here.

5-7 = 5 Earth strengthening (read: stimulating in a bad way) 7 Metal. The 7 Metal Star is representative of a person (young girl), body parts (teeth, mouth, jaw, breasts), and various deceitful acts or assault. So the 5 Star could stimulate any of these attributes in a negative way. You might think there is a huge difference between a 5-7 combination causing someone to have dental problems versus being pistol whipped and robbed. And you are correct. How could the 5-7 combination mean such drastically different things? There are other layers to Feng Shui, and the more you know about the total environment and who is occupying the space, the easier it is to narrow down the prediction of what might take place. Still, sometimes we cannot be 100% accurate or that specific. Metal is the solution to weaken the 5 Earth Star.

5-9 = 5 Earth being strengthened by 9 Fire. This is a really common Flying Star pattern, and most of the time it creates arguments in the household, set-backs, delays, pain, or accidents in a general context. Remember, there is no Trigram associated with the 5 Star, so there is no specific body area that is targeted. Looking at it another way, the 9 Star is the Li Trigram, which is associated with the heart or eyes. Since the 5 Star is a troublemaker, this could also indicate a potential for heart or eye problems. Metal is the cure here, and it is important not to have any Fire present with this combination.

6-1 = 6 Metal strengthening 1 Water. The meaning is almost identical to 1-6. The power and authority can nurture the wealth. Adding Earth to this area could strengthen the 6 Metal, which in turn will strengthen the 1 Water Star. But in certain circumstances you would add Water instead of Earth. First, get familiar with the basic meanings of the number combinations (Mountain Star and Water Star). Then you can eventually ponder the location of these Flying Stars, along with the other temporary influences. In other words, a 6-1 combination will behave differently in the North sector of a house versus the South sector. On top of that, any Annual Star will mix with the 6-1 combination and either enhance it or detract from it.

6-2 = 6 Metal being stimulated by 2 Earth. The possible outcome is head or lung problems, loneliness or detachment, sickness with the father figure. I once had a client who was taking care of her father with Alzheimer's disease. His bedroom was in the Northwest sector of the house (symbolic of the eldest man in the house). The Flying Stars in his room were 6-2. I met with her in 2007 when the Annual Star in his room was "3." Knowing that the following year in 2008 would bring an Annual 2 to the room, my prediction was that his health could worsen or that he could die in 2008. Of course, I recommended a truck load of Metal for his bedroom. The remedies do not always completely cancel out the negatives, but they absolutely help.

6-5 = 6 Metal being strengthened (read: irritated) by 5 Earth. I have emphasized the 6 Star being related to the father figure, but this Flying

Star combination can affect anyone. Since the 6 Star is related to the respiratory tract, it can cause problems in this region for anyone, including the numerous children who have allergies or asthma and use inhalers. Of course, smog and exposure to other airborne pollutants can affect our breathing, but the 6-5 Flying Stars can make things worse. Use Metal.

6-8 = 6 Metal being strengthened by 8 Earth. Here is an example of two Stars that are in a productive cycle together, and both Stars are considered inherently positive, even when they are not in a Wang phase. This combination can mean the occupant can be wealthy, powerful, and sometimes lonely. But it does not indicate any health problems, and this is one of the absolute best combinations of all the 81 different possibilities. Often, it is just good as is. Water or Fire can be added to stimulate the 8 Star further when it is in a Great Phase.

It is always important to know who is using a room like this. I once had a client whose teenage daughter was recovering from a massive head injury, which would handicap her for life, and she would likely have to live at home with her parents for many years. The girl's room was in a 6-8 section at the back middle portion of the house, which I wanted them to leave as is. But I do know that after clients have consultations with me, they often get so possessed by Feng Shui that they start trying to learn it on their own and go out to buy Feng Shui books.

In the 1990s the vast majority of Feng Shui books printed in English were from the Black Hat School, which recommends putting fire color in the back middle portion of the house. They call it the "fame" area. Knowing that this diluted version of Feng Shui is reckless with the elements, I made a big point of telling my client to resist putting any red color in her daughter's room, regardless of what she may hear or read. Although it may have been fine to put the Fire with the 8 Star, I did not see it being good at all with a 6 Metal Mountain Star in the bedroom of a person with a massive head injury. Remember, Fire destroys Metal. You may be wondering why such an awful accident happened to a girl in a 6-8 bedroom. The answer is that there were other Feng Shui influences outside her bedroom that contributed to this unfortunate event. The good news is that with a 6-8 Flying Star in the bedroom, the prospects for recovery are better, and it is like having guardian angels or good forces at work to compensate. Know that having good Feng Shui does not prevent all bad things from ever occurring.

The following floor plan in Fig. 3C was an interesting case study because of the unusual floor plan. One might think initially that a disjointed floor plan such as this one could harbor bad qi, and yet when the three separate sections of the house were gridded, it was revealed that the occupants enjoyed having the 8-6 and 6-8 Flying Stars at their garage entrance, their formal entrance, their home office desk location, and their master bedroom. And by no coincidence, these clients are financially very secure people.

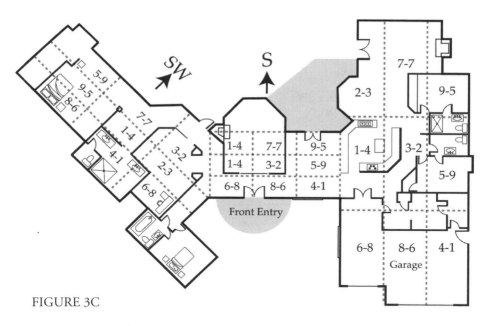

FIGURE 3C

7-1 = 7 Metal strengthening 1 Water. This energy pattern in a bedroom or entrance can signify that the occupants will be very social, fashion-conscious, and like to drink and entertain. I have been amused over the years to see how this is not only true, but also that sometimes the client even ends up having a bar or a wine collection right in the 7-1 area of the house. The woman might also have a voluminous wardrobe.

Twelve-steppers sometimes want to know how to control or weaken this tendency to indulge in their addictions, and the remedy is Wood. Wood weakens or drains the 1 Water Star, which is also symbolic of alcohol. Bring a large leafy plant into the 7-1 room and/or paint the walls green to lessen this influence.

7-2 = 7 Metal being strengthened by 2 Earth. The emphasis in this book is to compare the two most important stars, the Mountain Star and the Water Star. In some instances we also factor in the Period number. When the Period number 9 is added to a 7-2 or 2-7, then you have a combination that can indicate a house is prone to a literal fire. This could get triggered into reality if an Annual 5 Star joins the 2-7-9 combination. The remedy for this is completely outside the location of this Flying Star combination. And this would certainly be a surprise to learn about since in virtually every other instance you treat the problem right at the location where the Flying Stars exist. You can look up the chart in Chapter Four for a house that sits East 1 and was built in Period 5. You will see that the South section (South being inherently Fire) hosts a 7-2 combination with a Period 9 Star. So this house type is very prone to having a fire-related accident, especially in a heavily used room. Aside from putting Metal in this area, you can also go *outside* the house and put Water to the East, aligned with the East sector. By moistening the location of East (Zhen: Hard Wood) you can keep the house from catching fire.

7-5 = 7 Metal being strengthened by 5 Earth. The 7 Star is on the decline now, having been the Wang Star from 1984–2003. It was positive in Period 7, but its nature is negative in every other Period. With cheating, embezzlement, stealing, and betrayal as some of the 7 Star's character traits, and the 5 Star to antagonize it, this combination is best served with Metal and even some slow-moving Water. Metal will weaken the 5 Star, and slow-moving water can drain the 7 Metal. You do not want really fast-moving water here because it could stimulate the 5 Star too much. At the very least, add Metal.

7-8 = 7 Metal being strengthened by 8 Earth. The translation for this combination is "easy money." Things come easily for the little girl (7-Dui) and the little boy (8-Gen), like two kids playing together. No remedies are needed for this combination except in certain years. Some people look at this combination and add Water. Water drains the 7 Star and can also stimulate the 8 Star in Period 8.

8-6 = 8 Earth strengthens 6 Metal. It is a good timely Wang Star nurturing an old fading star that is inherently powerful but on the decline. No remedies needed except to deal with the occasional Annual Star.

8-7 = 8 Earth nurturing 7 Metal. This is a productive relationship in which the 8 Star is extremely positive right now in Period 8. This combination indicates easy wealth. The 8 Star will even be pretty good in Period 9 too. No remedies needed.

8-9 = 8 Earth being strengthened by 9 Fire. This is an extremely good combination and will be for a long time. I have a client who for many years was in an office with the 8-9 Flying Stars during Period 7. At that time, both the 8 and 9 Stars were in a Sheng Phase. Her business did very well, and she even became overwhelmed from having too much business. When I first met with her, I did not know how successful she already was, so I had suggested she have some maroon colored drapes in her office. Just as an interesting aside, she happens to be a landscape designer, so she has a special relationship with the earth, enhanced by the 8 Earth Star. After she added the red color to her office, her business increased even more, and she literally asked me what to do to slow things down. I told her to take away the red color, which she did, and things resumed back to a manageable level.

9-2 = 9 Fire strengthening 2 Earth. This combination, like the 2-9 arrangement, can indicate a number of problems usually related to the 2 Star more than the 9 Star. The 9 Star is often called an "intensifier" above and beyond it being the fire element. The 2-9 combination can cause bleeding, miscarriage, birth defects, and, completely separate from all that, depression or various illnesses for a man or woman. The 2 Star is the Kun Trigram, so it can also trigger digestion problems. Metal is usually added to weaken the 2 Star.

9-3 = 9 Fire being strengthened by 3 Wood. As described earlier in the 3-9 combination, the 3 Star can make someone rebellious, argumentative, gossipy, or vulnerable to legal problems. The gamut of legal problems can include any mishap or complication with a document or contract. This can include problems with insurance, immigration status, or anything to do with the government, like taxes. At the same time, it is entirely possible for the 9 Fire Star to "shine a light" on the eldest son in the family since the 3 Star is the Zhen Trigram, making him very successful at something at an early age, like a child actor or athlete. If you want to reduce the negative tendencies of the 3 Star, you can add more Fire. And here is another example where you would want to remove Water.

9-4 = 9 Fire is being strengthened by 4 Wood. Like the 4-9 combination, we have this potential for creative juices to be enhanced, as in art, music, writing, acting, or creating a product such as a jewelry line or some other design outlet. Even food catering could fall in this category of creativity. The 4 Star is very sexual and charged with social energy, so it supports any business that feeds the health and fitness industries. As well, the 4 Xun Star is associated with the legs and back. Sometimes the overlay of "coincidence" is really stunning in a Feng Shui analysis, such as finding the 4 Star at the entrance to a dance studio or a martial arts dojo or something to do with the lower back and legs, like a chiropractic office. This combination can be left as is, unless there are other influences, such as Annual Stars, which could necessitate Water or Fire.

9-5 = 9 Fire strengthening 5 Earth. Like the 5-9 combination, this is an example of Fire intensifying a Star that is in a bad phase for a long time. It can trigger or exacerbate problems related to the 5 or the 9 Star. Metal is the remedy.

9-8 = 9 Fire strengthening 8 Earth. This is a good combination, particularly in Period 8 as one of the best prosperity generating combinations. To increase that even further, you can add Fire.

DESTRUCTIVE STAR COMBINATIONS

1-2 = 1 Water being dominated by 2 Earth. In this case you look out for the element that is being dominated, which is Water. The remedy is Metal. Metal will weaken Earth and at the same time strengthen Water, all within the productive cycle of the elements. Otherwise, the 1-2 combination can cause problems with the kidneys, blood, circulation, or ears. As well, the 2 Star all by itself can trigger illness, loneliness, divorce, or separation. No red color here.

1-5 = 1 Water being dominated by 5 Earth. This element relationship is similar to the 1-2 combination. But the nature of the 5 Star creates different results. Here someone could be misdiagnosed. Perhaps that has something to do with the 5 Star indicating "delays." Someone could experience food poisoning or take the wrong medication, which poisons the blood. Taken further, the 1-5 combination can reveal when an occupant has a drug problem or, in some cases, sells drugs. Metal is the remedy.

1-8 = 1 Water being dominated by 8 Earth. Here we have an Earth Star controlling a Water Star, but these two Stars are considered inherently good. Sometimes this combination is left alone because the occupant can extract the positives out of each of these energies. But there is still a chance for this combination to create problems with the kidneys, blood, circulation, or ears. I have also seen a fair number of people with fibromyalgia in the 1-8 energy if it occurs in a place where someone spends a lot of time. Metal is the cure here.

1-9 = 1 Water dominating 9 Fire. Here we have to care about the Fire being extinguished with a negative result. The Li Trigram is associated with the eyes and heart, so it can reveal an occupant with vulnerabilities in these areas. Wood is the remedy because Water promotes Wood, and then Wood feeds Fire.

2-1 = 2 Earth dominates 1 Water. The remedy is Metal. This combination is very similar to the 1-2 combination, almost interchangeable. You can also look at the Stars for the Trigrams they represent. As Trigrams, you have the Kun (older woman) dominating the Kan (middle-aged man). Symbolically, it suggests that the woman in the house bosses the man around. Most men rebel against being controlled by a woman. This is why the 2-1 combination has the reputation for causing separation or divorce. Many times I have female clients who sleep in the 2-1 Stars, and not only do I recommend Metal as a cure, but I also recommend that they try to find a man who is secure and humble and who doesn't mind the woman taking charge or being powerful in the relationship.

2-3 = 2 Earth being dominated by 3 Wood. This combination is treated differently depending on other influences. Often, the annual energy will be the tie-breaker in terms of whether you add Fire or Metal to this combination. With strict Five-Element theory, you would add Fire to weaken the 3 Star and enhance the 2 Star. But you rarely want to enhance the 2 Star when it is in a bad phase. Instead, if you add Metal, it will dominate the 3 Wood and weaken (reduce) the 2 Earth. This combination is called the "fighting bull sha," and it can stimulate arguments, legal problems, and accidents.

2-4 = 2 Earth is dominated by 4 Wood. Like the 2-3 combination, it is rare that you would want to use the reductive cycle here because you do not want to strengthen the 2 Star until it goes into a good phase. There is, however, a special, non-obvious reason why you would strengthen the 2 Star. For a single man who enjoys having a lot of girl-friends or sexual conquests, adding Fire here can encourage his prospects even further. This, however, works in the opposite way for a woman who dwells in the 2-4 Star combination. Adding Fire to this combination could make a woman be the victim of an unfaithful lover. Metal would be the cure for this combination, especially if a married couple had these Flying Stars in their bedroom.

3-2 = 3 Wood dominates 2 Earth. This combination is virtually identical in meaning to the 2-3 arrangement. Metal is usually the cure to help prevent legal woes, arguments or accidents.

3-5 = 3 Wood dominating 5 Earth. Keep in mind that the 5 Star will just irritate whatever it is around when it is in a bad phase. The 3 Wood Star is also the Zhen Trigram. Zhen attributes can be affected, such as the eldest son being more argumentative or accident-prone. This could also give someone problems with their feet, throat, thyroid, or nervous system. The 3-5 combination also seems to match up with people who complain of on-going, changing ailments. We call them hypochondriacs. Since the 3 Star is also related to hysteria and convulsions, I do think there are modern-day ailments and mental illnesses that can be triggered in a 3-5 environment, including bipolar disorders or schizophrenia.

3-6 = 3 Wood being dominated by 6 Metal. Some schools indicate that this is just a positive Star controlling a negative Star (in Periods 6, 7, and 8) and that you can leave it alone. This is a combination you might remedy with Water or Fire, depending on whether you want to control or strengthen the 3 Star. Often, you will want to suppress the 3 Star with Fire since it can attract arguments or legal problems. But if this domination cycle is causing someone to have problems with their feet, throat, or nervous system, then you would want to strengthen it with Water instead.

3-7 = 3 Wood being dominated by 7 Metal. Here you have the same element combination as the 3-6 Star just described. But the 3-7 combination is specifically called the "robbery star" combination, and it is usually controlled with Fire. This is an instance where you want to cancel out the whole equation. Fire will weaken the 3 Wood Star, and it will dominate the 7 Metal Star. Otherwise, this combination has a reputation for causing people to be vulnerable to theft, literal theft as well as contractual and financial betrayal.

3-8 = 3 Wood dominating 8 Earth. In Period 8 we don't want to see the 8 Star under pressure by being dominated by a Wood Star. This could suppress a person's potential for wealth, and it could be complicated by legal issues. Add Fire. This combination can also be bad for young people and undermine the ability to conceive.

4-2 = 4 Wood dominating 2 Earth. This Star combination has some very non-obvious definitions. Even though the 4 Star is associated with the Xun Trigram (eldest daughter in the family structure), the 4 Star in this combination can also represent a man. And the man is controlling the woman. When a man spends a lot of time in the 4-2 Stars, he can be very charismatic and have a lot of girlfriends. I have a friend who moved into a house where her thirteen-year-old son had a bedroom in the 4-2 area of their house. Previously, the kid could have been classified as kind of nerdy. I told her to watch out, that her son would become a "chick magnet." And that did happen rather quickly. He was six feet tall by the time he was fourteen and looked older than he was. And he became quite popular with the girls.

In contrast, when a woman spends a lot of time in the 4-2 Stars, it can imply that her own boyfriend or husband will not be faithful. For a man, you can leave the 4-2 combination alone or add Fire to strengthen the 2 (which stands for a woman), and it will bring even more women to the man. But a woman who dwells in the 4-2 Stars usually wants to cancel them out with Metal. If you look at the 4-2 combination as Trigrams, it is the Xun (eldest daughter) and the Kun Trigram (mother). This combination can also mean the mother-in-law and daughter-in-law do not get along. This is particularly interesting because it is an example of how a circumstance can exist and be defined with Feng Shui even when the two women are not living in the same house. Of course, this would be intensified if they were living in the same house.

4-5 = 4 Wood dominating 5 Earth. The 5 Star is not related to any particular body organ, but it is associated with the skin. If the 4 Wood Star is putting pressure on the 5 Earth Star, then a skin problem can result. The antagonism goes the other way as well. Since 5 is an irritant to whatever it is around, it can "attack" the 4 Star, associated with the back and legs, giving a person problems in that area. Metal can knock out the troublemaker here, the 5 Earth Star.

4-6 = 4 Wood being dominated by 6 Metal. In this instance you usually want to help the 4 Wood Star with Water. Even though the 4 Star is in a bad phase right now, it still possesses some good qualities. If a person is struggling in his or her career and creativity, then you might want to support the 4 Star with Water. As well, the 4-6 combination can cause back or leg problems, for which Water is again the cure. One thing to remember, whether a Star is in a good or bad phase, is that if it is being dominated by another Star, then its worst characteristics will become manifest.

4-7 = 4 Wood being dominated by 7 Metal. Here you have a very similar configuration to the 4-6 Stars combination. It is the same elements in a domination cycle with the 4 Star being oppressed. Above and beyond the domination cycle, I have sometimes noticed that the 4 and 7 Stars show up together in places that emanate a lot of sexuality. The 4 Star is the Xun Trigram, and the 7 Star is the Dui Trigram. It is the eldest daughter who is very independent and the youngest daughter who is very flirty. I had a client once with a stripper-for-hire business. I normally wouldn't do a reading for someone with a stripper business, and I was deceived a little before I showed up at the location (another aspect of the 7 Star at work!). I thought I was going to an "exotic cake company" but was later told that the business was a party stripper booking agency. Its entrance was the 4-7 combination, and the head of the company had her office in the 7-1 Stars. I have been to a few other businesses that focused on female sexuality, and the 4-7 Stars were prominently placed in the floor plan. Remember, the 4 Star is related to such body parts as the hips, buttocks, and thighs. The 7 Star is related to the mouth and the breasts. Need I say more?

4-8 = 4 Wood dominating 8 Earth. Like the 3-8 combination, the goal here is to liberate the 8 Star from its oppression and enhance it with Fire. Then it can be an especially creative area that helps people make money. It could be a great area for a writer. Without the presence of Fire, this combination can influence people similarly to the 8-4 combination, which can trigger miscarriages or attract harm to children.

5-1 = 5 Earth dominating 1 Water. Here you want to help or strengthen Water because it represents wealth and affluence. At the same time, you want to weaken the 5 Earth because by itself the 5 Star can trigger arguments or accidents. Metal is the cure. Since the 1 Water Star also represents kidneys, blood, circulation, and ears, this 5-1 combination can also indicate health problems in these areas, as well as that one has been misdiagnosed or is taking the wrong medication. In reality, the blood gets poisoned when the wrong medicine is taken.

5-3 = 5 Earth being dominated by 3 Wood. This combination is usually remedied with Metal, except in Period 5. The 5 is an irritant to all things "zhen." The 3 Star is related to the eldest son and the body areas of the feet, throat, nervous system, and liver. This combination can also signal a hypochondriac because the yearly and monthly influences seem to have more of an effect on this combination.

5-4 = 5 Earth being dominated by 4 Wood. Here you can also look at the 5 irritating the 4 Star and causing Xun-related problems. The 5-4 combination can also contribute to rheumatism or skin problems. Metal is the remedy. Often, you can use a lot of Metal for some 5 combinations. But with the 5-4 combination, you can use *less* Metal so as not to cause excessive domination of the 4 Star.

6-3 = 6 Metal dominating 3 Wood. What you do with this combination might depend on its location, such as an entrance versus a bedroom. With an entrance you would be more concerned with the Water Star 3. With a bedroom you would be more concerned with the Mountain Star 6. Also, you might actually want to strengthen the 3 Star if the person using the room is the Zhen Trigram based on their birth year. Otherwise, Fire would be the cure to weaken the 3 Star's negative effects.

6-4 = 6 Metal dominating 4 Wood. Here you would most likely add Water to strengthen the 4 so that the body areas associated with the 4 Star are not under pressure or vulnerable to injury. For example, since the 4 Star is related to the hips and pelvic region, this would *not* be a good area for a pregnant woman to spend a lot of time.

6-9 = 6 Metal being dominated by 9 Fire. Here you add Earth to strengthen the 6 Metal. Otherwise, Qian-related problems come out, such as head or lung ailments.

Also, this combination can indicate that the man in the house or the father is under pressure and not respected by the children in the house. This combination can get compounded even further if it happens to be in the Northwest part of the house and/or the kitchen. The kitchen contains the stove (Fire), so it just brings more of the harmful element into play.

7-3 = 7 Metal dominating 3 Wood. This is the robbery star combination where the whole equation needs to be canceled out, usually with Fire. Fire weakens Wood and destroys Metal. So Fire is the remedy to control this combination.

7-4 = 7 Metal dominates 4 Wood. This combination is similar to the 6-4 Stars. Water is usually added to strengthen the 4 Wood. Both of these Stars are "unfavorable" in Period 8 and for many Periods to come. It might be appropriate in some instances to treat this combination more like 7-3 and add Fire. For example, with both the 4 and 7 Stars capable of causing infidelity or sexual scandal, it might become appropriate to cancel out the whole equation instead of strengthening the 4 Star. This is why it is so important to know who is occupying these spaces. If that person is struggling to be an actor or to write a book, I would still think to strengthen the 4 Star with Water. But if the person is complaining about all his or her heartache in matters of love and being cheated on, then I would suggest Fire instead.

7-9 = 7 Metal being dominated by 9 Fire. This combination can bring out the worst in the 7 Star, so Earth is usually added to mitigate all the pressure of this domination cycle. Without Earth, the 7-9 Stars could cause problems with the teeth, mouth, jaw, lips, gums, or breasts.

8-1 = 8 Earth dominates 1 Water. Here we have two good Stars in Period 8 that happen to form a domination cycle. Depending on whether you want to emphasize the Mountains Star or the Water Star, you would either add Fire, Metal, or maybe just leave things alone. If someone in this space is experiencing "kan"-related problems, then you would want to add some Metal to strengthen the 1 Water Star.

8-3 = 8 Earth being dominated by 3 Wood. The 8 Star is an inherently good Star and is the king of all Stars in Period 8, so it needs to be supported with Fire. Here it can prevent bone or muscle problems, joint or hand pain, or fertility issues. The 8-3 Stars can cause children to have injuries or problems with their limbs. I've even seen this manifest with kids who grow so quickly their bones ache or they develop spinal problems. In the house I grew up in, my older sister's bedroom straddled the 4-8 and 8-3 sections of the house. Aside from having both real and self-induced pressure on her as she grew up, her posture was so bad that at one point my mother wanted to put her in a back brace.

8-4 = 8 Earth being dominated by 4 Wood. This is a very similar combination and effect to the 8-3 Stars. And *both* combinations can place pressure on a child and undermine fertility. Hand problems also manifest with the 8-4 Star influence. Fire is the answer.

9-1 = 9 Fire being dominated by 1 Water. Both of these Stars are positive in Period 8 and Period 9. The 9 Star represents the heart and eyes, so to strengthen the 9 Fire Star, you can use Wood (a live plant). A very large display of green color can also be used to represent wood.

9-6 = 9 Fire dominating 6 Metal. This combination can be almost identical to the definition given for 6-9. The subtle difference is that 6 on the Water Star side could affect someone more professionally whereas 6 on the Mountain Star side might affect someone more in terms of health. Earth is the cure.

9-7 = 9 Fire dominating 7 Metal. This combination probably requires Earth most of the time, but there could be an argument for using actual water to reduce the 7 Star when it is in the Water Star position. The cure for this combination also depends on its location because the inherent energy of the location can make a difference. For instance, a 9-7 combination in the South (inherently a Fire direction) is more likely to require Earth than a 9-7 combination in the Northwest (inherently associated with Metal). Just know that the inherent element associated with a direction is like a shadow influence on the Mountain and Water Stars.

SAME STAR AND ELEMENT COMBINATIONS

1-1 = Double Water. When the 1 Star is in a good phase, this can mean wealth and other positive attributes. The 1 Star is also representative of the Kan Trigram, which is the middle son symbolically in the family structure. This 1-1 combination can also indicate the occupants could be gay men. Since very few Feng Shui books make mention of circumstances that reflect a person's sexual orientation, I only present this information as another example of how specific and personal Feng Shui can be. The state of someone being gay or straight is not to be considered good or bad. It is just a fact of life and a variation in biology. We have Star combinations that address other areas of human sexuality and relationship scenarios, and this is just one of them.

2-2 = Double Earth. The definition all depends on what cycle the 2 Stars are in. When they are in a great phase, the 2 Star is a wealth Star, and it always relates to Earth, so it can indicate someone who owns a lot of land. But in a bad phase it can indicate the occupant could be very lonely and sickly. You would add Fire to enhance the 2-2 combination in a good or great phase but weaken with Metal when the 2 Star is in a bad phase, such as in Period 8.

2-5 = Double Earth, but each Star has some negative connotations. The two of them together create a potential for great disaster, mishap, arguments, or pain. It is one of the most critical number combinations, and a lot of Metal is advised. Consultants have different opinions on whether certain types of metal are superior to others, such as copper versus iron. As well, some claim that metal must be exposed to the majority of the air in a room to work. I have seen that hidden metal can work as well as exposed metal. So, if someone wanted to hide fifty pounds of iron weights under their child's bed, I know it can work, even as it is tucked out of the child's way.

2-8 = Double Earth, but we have a real mixed message here. These two Stars are never good at the same time, so it can usually mean the occupant will be wealthy but not healthy. A little Metal is used. In order to protect health, some Metal will have to be used at the expense of the combination's wealth potential. We must also remember that the 8 Star is symbolic of children in general or a young boy more specifically. In Period 8, when the 2 Star enters the center palace, as in 2007, there is a greater tendency for children to have sicknesses. This is just an example of how a Period Star combined with an annual influence can predict something that might occur in the general population. Literally, as I was adding this very sentence to the book, the evening news (August 17, 2007) reported that millions of children's toys were being recalled in the United States out of concern for their lead content.

3-3 = Double Wood. Again, you have to know whether to suppress the 3 Stars with Fire or to enhance with Water when the 3 Star is in a Wang phase. The interpretation can vary from extreme wealth and no-bility (master of pen and sword) to the potential for criminal activity when the 3 Star is in a bad phase, such as in Periods 8 and 9.

3-4 = Hard Wood and Soft Wood combined. It is representative of the eldest son (Zhen) and the eldest daughter (Xun). When they get together, you have this sort of incestuous mixture of creativity and cra-ziness. If the person using a room with the 3-4 combination is at all emotionally unstable, then this number combination could push him or her over the edge. It is usually good to suppress this combination with Fire, unless there is an Annual (visiting 5 or 2 Star). When an annual 5 or 2 Star comes to visit this combination, you should take away Fire except for when the 2 or 5 Star is in a good phase.

4-3 = This is the same Star combination listed above, but there is a reversal of the Mountain Star and Water Star positions. It is usually a distinction without a difference. Add Fire most of the time. This could indicate a creative person who is plagued by legal issues or gossip. It might also indicate a very sexual person who is rebellious and argumentative. Although it takes a while to memorize all the Star combination and their other influences, try always to be mindful of the family members and body areas associated with the Trigrams. It is also insightful to look at the age and occupation of someone who dwells in any given Flying Star combination. Often these Star combinations will reflect, help, or hinder certain businesses. If the entrance doors to the *National Enquirer* publication were a 4-3 combination, that would be highly appropriate (sex and gossip).

4-4 = Double 4 Wood. It can suggest a place that is highly supportive of the arts or academia. You could add Water or Fire depending on the Period. Also, you might change your remedy to accommodate a visiting Annual Star. The 4-4 Stars can provide a great entrance for a restaurant, night club, dance place, music store, book store, art gallery, school, travel agency, retail clothing or manufacturing store, design, hair, or nail salon or any type of beauty or health center. The 4 Star caters to health, youth, beauty, travel, sexuality, the arts, and philosophy. This is one reason I just have to laugh whenever someone asks me about how and why the number 4 is supposed to symbolize bad luck in Feng Shui. This question comes up very often because the Chinese do not like the word for the number 4 in Mandarin. It sounds very similar to their word for death, so there is a cultural association with the number 4 that has little to do with the Xun Trigram and Feng Shui calculations.

Still, I see the perpetuation of this myth when poorly-trained Feng Shui authors state that having a 4 in your address is unlucky.

5-2 = Double Earth. This combination is virtually identical to the 2-5 combination where you add Metal as a cure. But there is one type of Metal you do not want to add to this 2 and 5 combination. You do not want to add a 6-rod metal wind chime because there is something truly bizarre about the 2/5/6 combination. It can attract a ghost. So, have any *other* type of metal besides a metal wind chime with the 5-2 or 2-5 Flying Stars. You could have a grandfather clock or some heavy pieces of metal, just no wind chime in that 5-2 area. If your house has a 5-2 or 2-5 combination and you hang a metal wind chime somewhere around the house that is not near the 2-5 area, then you are okay to use the chime without it attracting a ghost.

5-5 = Double Earth. You will not see a 5-5 combination in an advanced Flying Star chart because there are no double facing or double sitting house types from Period 5. You would only see a 5-5 combination if it were with other stars, like a 5 Mountain Star joined by an Annual 5 Star. Since the 5 Star is singularly a dangerous energy (when not in a 5 Wang Cycle), a double combination of it is as bad as the 2-5 combination.

5-8 = 5 Earth matching 8 Earth. This is a mixed message where you need to be concerned that the 5 Star will be irritating to the 8 Star when we are not in Period 5. This could cause bone or muscle problems. This could also put pressure on the boy in the house. If this Star combination is in a bedroom, you should add a little Metal to weaken the 5 Mountain Star.

6-6 = Double Metal. This is a double dose of hard metal, the Qian Trigram. This represents "clashing swords," and it can indicate power struggles, injury by a metal object, or the potential for violence. It can also just mean that the head of the house is very strong. One funny manifestation of the 6-6 combination showing up in the South section of the house (inherently Fire), especially if it is a kitchen (with a stove also creating fire), is that the man in the house will be bald. How on earth can you get that kind of information from a 6-6 combination in the South? It is very subtle, but since the Qian Trigram represents the head, when it combines with a fiery location, we say the fire burns the hair off the top of the head, thus resulting in a balding man. Weird but true!

The 6-6 combination can represent self-defense or authority. So it is not bad to have a 6-6 combination at the entrance to a government building, a martial arts studio, or a place representing something powerful and authoritative like a police station. Most Feng Shui books make a reference to how bad it is to have a front door aligned with an oncoming street, but if the 6-6 combination is there, we say it can handle the force of the qi. The Qian Trigram is Hard Metal. It can, like a shield, handle the qi coming toward it and even turn it into something good. I have a client who owns a business location, the entrance of which faces a T-juncture. The 6-6 combination is there at the entrance, and I did not hesitate to recommend this commercial space to him. He is very successful in that location. The 6-6 combination can also mean the occupants may argue a lot, so the remedy would be to soften or weaken the heavy metal combination with Water.

6-7 = Double Metal. This combination is also quite strong as Soft Metal and Hard Metal combined. In Period 7 it was customary to keep these Stars strong and fortify them with Earth cures. But in Period 8, it is more common to want to weaken these double metal Stars with Water so that they do not contribute to injuries or clashes.

7-6 = Double Metal. See above. They are almost identical in their influence.

7-7 = Double Metal. Going back to the fact that the 7 Star is the Dui Trigram and related to the image of a young and sexy female, this 7-7 combination can still be good for a female embarking on a career in modeling, singing, or acting. It helps support nighttime businesses like night clubs and bars. But when the 7 Star is not in a good phase, it can bring on deception, betrayal, embezzlement, theft, and assault. What you do with this 7-7 combination will depend on other influences. For example, when an Annual 3 Star joins the group, you would treat it as a mini robbery star combination and add Fire. But if an Annual 7 joined the 7-7 Stars, that is way too much Metal, and you would probably want to use Water to reduce the excessive metal qi.

8-2 = Double Earth. See the description for the 2-8 combination. Often, these number combinations will have a similar effect whether one number is in the Mountain Star position or switched to the Water Star position. Where you would have the biggest difference is if these combinations were in the center palace. The Center Stars will reveal whether a house is in a "Locked Period," a topic that will be discussed in an upcoming chapter. In Locked Periods, you will want to pay close attention to the Mountain and Water Stars to determine what kind of Locked Period it is. This 8-2 combination could indicate some sickness, especially to the bones or muscles. Add Metal.

8-5 = Double Earth. Like the 5-8 combination, you will need to add a little Metal to control the 5, but it is at the expense of also reducing the 8 prosperity Star.

8-8 = Double Earth. This is one of the best combinations possible because it only occurs when the house is built in Period 8, making the 8 Stars even more positive than they are in Period 6, 7, or 9. Sometimes it is just good to leave this combination alone. Adding Fire can make it even more active for generating money luck.

9-9 = Double Fire. This combination is extreme, and the interpretation has everything to do with what Period we are currently living in. In Period 9, this combination is going to be quite positive, but fast-forward a few Periods and the 9-9 combination has more than a century of being a really negative area that could cause mental problems for the occupants, accidents, and fire-related problems. Earth would be used to weaken this combination while Wood is used to enhance it. Feng Shui practitioners in Period 9 will be recommending a lot more indoor plants to enhance the 9 Star than they did in previous Periods!

USING THE REDUCTIVE ELEMENT

Using the reductive element is usually the first choice when you have a domination of two elements. It is the most sophisticated way to remedy a domination cycle and sometimes even a productive combination of Stars if you don't like what they mean. So, as you learned from the Flying Star combination section, if you want to support a good Star that is being dominated (like 4-8), then use the reductive cycle element for the 4-8 combination, which is Fire. Additionally, if you don't like the meaning of a same-element combination like 2-5, then you should still add the reductive element of Metal to weaken *both* of the Earth Stars.

USING THE DESTRUCTIVE ELEMENT

Using a destructive element (which can be reductive to one of the Stars) is sometimes the only thing you can do. Examples were given such as the 3-2 and 2-3 combinations or the 4-5 and 5-4 combinations. You just have to weaken both of the Stars in order to cancel out the potential problems associated with the Star combination.

MOUNTAIN STARS IN YIN ROOMS

I have seen that some of the Star combinations behave similarly regardless of the order of the Stars, such as 4-8 and 8-4. But generally speaking, the Mountain Star will relate more to health and relationships and the Water Star more to career. If you have an 8-4 Star combination in a bedroom, which is a yin room, then you would pay more attention to the Mountain Star influence.

WATER STARS IN YANG ROOMS

Water Stars in yang areas of a house will have slightly more influence than Mountain Stars. So, at a front door, a 5-8 combination is pretty good for an entrance because the 8 Water Star will be more influential than the Mountain Star.

This does not mean you don't use Metal, but you can say that a 5-8 combination at a front door is a little better than an 8-5 combination at the front door (in Period 8).

For those of you who already know how to float Annual Stars, this information is very relevant because it will help you know what element to add to an area when it appears that there is a contradiction between the Mountain Star and Water Star.

To illustrate the point: Let us say you have a 4-6 combination at an entrance and then a 9 Annual Star joins them. You can place more emphasis on the 9 Annual Star affecting the 6 Water Star. This forms a mini 9-6 combination, so you would use Earth as a remedy.

Compare that to a 4-6 combination in a bedroom with an annual 8 Star joining them. Here you would pay more attention to how the 8 Annual Star affects the 4 Mountain Star and might choose to use Fire to correct the mini 8-4 combination.

WHEN TO INCLUDE THE PERIOD STAR OR ANNUAL STAR WITH THE MOUNTAIN AND WATER STARS

The emphasis in this book is on the relationship between the Mountain Star and Water Star because those are the most influential Stars. Then an annual influence will also act like a trigger for something to happen. The Period Star is sometimes taken into consideration, and there will be some House Type examples in the next chapter that show all three Stars forming a trilogy of meaning. Other examples of putting three or more Stars together include the following:

- A 2-7 combination with a Period 9 Star can indicate a house type or location in a house prone to a fire.
- If a house has the Stars 2, 4, 7, and 9 in the bedrooms in the Southwest, Southeast, West, and South, then this will be a house with lots of gossip. It can also be a house type that easily harbors a ghost.
- A 2-5 at the entrance or master bedroom with an Annual 5 can indicate the man will become a widower.

- A 5-2 at the entrance or master bedroom with an Annual 2 can indicate the woman will become a widow.

  (Master Sang said that if you do not want to become a widow or widower that year, then you can move a relative or housekeeper into the house who *is* already a widow or widower, and it will prevent you from becoming one yourself.... This is just one example of how another human being can become a Feng Shui remedy.)

- A 7-9 combination with a Period 5 Star can indicate the occupant's potential for surgery. The Period 5 Star or even an Annual 5 Star can do this, especially when this trilogy occurs in the bedroom or at the entrance.

- A 7-9 combination with a Period 4 star can indicate the man in the house is vulnerable to contracting an STD. In a Reversed House, the 7-9-4 combination can also indicate a potential for a fire.

- A 1-6 combination with a Period 8 is a wonderful trilogy of inherently good Stars that can indicate long-lasting or easy prosperity.

- When the 1, 6, and 8 Stars are found in the entrance, kitchen, and master bedroom, they can indicate a good house for both money and having kids.

- Just note that the Period Star can intensify the Mountain Star or Water Star. You don't apply a remedy specifically to the Period Star, but it can further irritate a Mountain Star or Water Star. An example of that is a 1-5 combination with a Period 5 Construction Star. That would be worse than a 1-5 combination with a Period 8 Construction Star.

- One more common Star combination, 4-6, can also have a rare but intense implication when it is in the east or southeast sector. The 6 Star relates to the head, and the 4 Star is also symbolic of a snake. The snake can also be symbolic of a rope. When you put a rope and a head together, there is a rare possibility of a hanging. If other negative forces are in place, including the Fire element in this area, then it can trigger such a tragedy. The Fire element could manifest in the form of a car's headlights. If a house is positioned on a corner or a T-juncture and there are nightly trails of headlights flashing onto a section of a house with bad Stars, this can create the Fire sha.

I once had a client who was perfecting an elaborate landscape design when we met. It was to include floodlights to showcase some trees near the master bedroom window with a 4-6 combination inside the east sector. For the very reason mentioned above, I recommended that the floodlights be positioned *away* from the house instead of toward it. This client is a famous actor, and he had already had a friend die a tragic death on one of his properties. At the time, this actor dabbled in drugs, and I got a little spooked with how he had this potentially dangerous combination of Feng Shui influences going on at his home. I did not tell him why there should be no lights shining on the 4-6 area, but I wrote in the report that it could cause some accidents and that the outside lighting should be altered.

CHAPTER FOUR

The Four Major House Types

For all the house type charts listed in this chapter, the orientation reference is for the back side of the house, referred to as the sitting side. A chart that says a house "sits" in a particular direction indicates that as the back side, presumably the opposite of the facing side, which is the front. A house that "sits" North means it faces South.

All of the following house type charts have been arranged to have the sitting side of the house chart toward the bottom of each page. The arrow ^ symbol represents a facing direction. All of the boxy charts can be superimposed over real floor plans.

The reason a house is defined according to its sitting side and not its facing side is because the back of a house is like its spine. The real strength and character of a house comes from its back in the same way that your spine holds your head and torso up.

WANG SHAN WANG SHUI: ALSO KNOWN AS DAO SHAN DAO XIANG

This is one of four major house types and is considered, in a general way, to be the best of the four. "Wang" means "strong," and "shan" means "mountain." The mountain energy is symbolic of people in their health and relationships. "Shui" means water, literally, and more sym-

97

bolically prosperity. So the house that is inherently good for people and good for money is often a sought-after house type. "Dao Shan Dao Xiang" can be translated : "The mountain has arrived; the facing has arrived (in their correct locations)."

This house type does not need any remedies on the outside to balance it out because it is already balanced. If the Wang Shan Wang Shui house sits on flat land, then it is considered stable. But this house is considered even better, and more supported by the outside environment, when there is higher land behind it and lower land level on the facing side.

FIGURE 4A is of a house with higher land behind it and lower in front.

Higher land can literally be a hill or mountain behind the house, but it could also be a taller man-made structure. If you live in a one-story house and your neighbor behind you is in a two-story house, that can be considered a mountain. Lower land level need only be a couple feet lower to qualify as the "virtual water." Some people even think that a few inches lower is enough to make a difference. So, let it be clear that the Wang Shan Wang Shui house does not have to have a mountain behind it and virtual water or real water in front of it. But if you want to put a fountain in front of the Wang Shan Wang Shui house, it would make a good house even better for money luck.

What happens when a Wang Shan Wang Shui house has the opposite formations around it? By this, I mean water on the sitting side and a mountain on the facing side. Well, it undermines the house a bit. It doesn't totally ruin it or make it not a Wang Shan Wang Shui house; it just takes it down a notch. I sometimes feel that the Wang Shan Wang Shui house is a bit overrated. Sure, it is a good feature to start with, and I never ignore its status when I am evaluating a house for clients, whether they already live in the house or plan to move into it. But I have also seen this house type *not* live up to its name because of other overriding features. I have to emphasize this fact *because many people learn a little Feng Shui and they think that the Wang Shan Wang Shui house makes the occupants immune to problems, and this is far from the truth.*

The overriding circumstance that could ruin or undermine a Wang Shan Wang Shui house is negative Flying Stars in the bedrooms or at the entrance or any other important area of the house such as a home office. For example, if you were to ask me which I prefer, a Wang Shan Wang Shui house with a 5-9 master bedroom or a lesser house type (to be discussed later) with an 8-6 or 8-8 master bedroom, I would prefer to live in the one with the best Flying Stars in the master bedroom. This is because we spend a third of our lives in the bedroom. If you lived in a lesser house type but had great energy in your bedroom, it might be like living in the best neighborhood in your not-so great city as opposed to living in a crummy neighborhood in a rich city.

Other overriding features could include something overwhelmingly bad in the immediate exterior environment, a really confusing floor plan, or an extreme imbalance of yin-yang energies. So, in other words, if a Wang Shan Wang Shui house is shaped like a boomerang, sitting at the bottom of a canyon, and perpetually dark all the time, I would say "no thank you" to that Wang Shan Wang Shui house.

I should also say that the status of a Wang Shan Wang Shui house becomes more valuable in a commercial setting or an apartment complex, where the occupant may have no control over the exteriors. It would be one less thing to worry about. How do you identify a Wang Shan Wang Shui house type chart? After you have done your calculations on the house, as explained in Chapter Two, look to the sitting and facing palaces on the chart. The sitting palace (back middle sector) will have a set of numbers, which are called the sitting number and the facing number for that sector. They are also called the Mountain Star and the Water Star for that sitting sector.

If the number in the sitting position (to the left of the hyphen) matches the Construction Cycle number of the house (aka Period Star), then you have the "wang shan" status of the house determined. Then, the "wang shui" status would be revealed by looking at the facing palace (front middle sector). If the Water Star or "money number" matches the Period Star of the house, that is considered the ideal placement. Example: 5-9 in the sitting and 1-5 in the facing would reveal a Wang Shan Wang Shui chart for a house built in Period 5.

CHARTS FOR THE
WANG SHAN WANG SHUI HOUSE TYPES

Period 1
There are no Wang Shan Wang Shui House Types in Period 1

Period 2
Sits NE 1

∧

S 1-4 6	SW 8-2 8	W 3-6 4
SE 6-9 1	5-8 2	NW 4-7 3
E 7-1 9	NE 2-5 5	N 9-3 7

Sits SW 1

∧

N 3-9 7	NE 5-2 5	E 1-7 9
NW 7-4 3	8-5 2	SE 9-6 1
W 6-3 4	SW 2-8 8	S 4-1 6

Sits SE 2 or 3

∧

W 8-1 4	NW 9-2 3	N 5-7 7
SW 4-6 8	1-3 2	NE 7-9 5
S 6-8 6	SE 2-4 1	E 3-5 9

Sits NW 2 or 3

∧

E 5-3 9	SE 4-2 1	S 8-6 6
NE 9-7 5	3-1 2	SW 6-4 8
N 7-5 7	NW 2-9 3	W 1-8 4

Period 3
Sits West 2 or 3

^

NE 2-7	E 7-3	SE 6-2
6	1	2
N 9-5	5-1	S 1-6
8	3	7
NW 4-9	W 3-8	SW 8-4
4	5	9

Sits East 2 or 3

^

SW 4-8	W 8-3	NW 9-4
9	5	4
S 6-1	1-5	N 5-9
7	3	8
SE 2-6	E 3-7	NE 7-2
2	1	6

Sits SE 1

^

W 9-2	NW 1-3	N 6-8
5	4	8
SW 5-7	2-4	NE 8-1
9	3	6
S 7-9	SE 3-5	E 4-6
7	2	1

Sits NW 1

^

E 6-4	SE 5-3	S 9-7
1	2	7
NE 1-8	4-2	SW 7-5
6	3	9
N 8-6	NW 3-1	W 2-9
8	4	5

Period 4
Sits SW 2 or 3

∧

N 5-2 9	NE 7-4 7	E 3-9 2
NW 9-6 5	1-7 4	SE 2-8 3
W 8-5 6	SW 4-1 1	S 6-3 8

Sits NE 2 or 3

∧

S 3-6 8	SW 1-4 1	W 5-8 6
SE 8-2 3	7-1 4	NW 6-9 5
E 9-3 2	NE 4-7 7	N 2-5 9

Sits West 1

∧

NE 3-8 7	E 8-4 2	SE 7-3 3
N 1-6 9	6-2 4	S 2-7 8
NW 5-1 5	W 4-9 6	SW 9-5 1

Sits East 1

∧

SW 5-9 1	W 9-4 6	NW 1-5 5
S 7-2 8	2-6 4	N 6-1 9
SE 3-7 3	E 4-8 2	NE 8-3 7

Period 5
Sits SW 1

∧

N 6-3	NE 8-5	E 4-1
1	8	3
NW 1-7	2-8	SE 3-9
6	5	4
W 9-6	SW 5-2	S 7-4
7	2	9

Sits South 2 or 3

∧

NW 8-9	N 4-5	NE 6-7
6	1	8
W 7-8	9-1	E 2-3
7	5	3
SW 3-4	S 5-6	SE 1-2
2	9	4

Sits North 2 or 3

∧

SE 2-1	S 6-5	SW 4-3
4	9	2
E 3-2	1-9	W 8-7
3	5	7
NE 7-6	N 5-4	NW 9-8
8	1	6

Sits NE 1

∧

S 4-7	SW 2-5	W 6-9
9	2	7
SE 9-3	8-2	NW 7-1
4	5	6
E 1-4	NE 5-8	N 3-6
3	8	1

Sits West 2 or 3

∧

NE 4-9 8	E 9-5 3	SE 8-4 4
N 2-7 1	7-3 5	S 3-8 9
NW 6-2 6	W 5-1 7	SW 1-6 2

Sits East 2 or 3

∧

SW 6-1 2	W 1-5 7	NW 2-6 6
S 8-3 9	3-7 5	N 7-2 1
SE 4-8 4	E 5-9 3	NE 9-4 8

Sits NW 1

∧

E 8-6 3	SE 7-5 4	S 2-9 9
NE 3-1 8	6-4 5	SW 9-7 2
N 1-8 1	NW 5-3 6	W 4-2 7

Sits SE 1

∧

W 2-4 7	NW 3-5 6	N 8-1 1
SW 7-9 2	4-6 5	NE 1-3 8
S 9-2 9	SE 5-7 4	E 6-8 3

Period 6
Sits SW 2 or 3

∧

N 7-4 2	NE 9-6 9	E 5-2 4
NW 2-8 7	3-9 6	SE 4-1 5
W 1-7 8	SW 6-3 3	S 8-5 1

Sits NE 2 or 3

∧

S 5-8 1	SW 3-6 3	W 7-1 8
SE 1-4 5	9-3 6	NW 8-2 7
E 2-5 4	NE 6-9 9	N 4-7 2

Sits West 1

∧

NE 5-1 9	E 1-6 4	SE 9-5 5
N 3-8 2	8-4 6	S 4-9 1
NW 7-3 7	W 6-2 8	SW 2-7 3

Sits East 1

∧

SW 7-2 3	W 2-6 8	NW 3-7 7
S 9-4 1	4-8 6	N 8-3 2
SE 5-9 5	E 6-1 4	NE 1-5 9

Period 7
Sits West 2 or 3

<table>
<tr><td colspan="3" align="center">∧</td></tr>
<tr><td>NE 6-2
1</td><td>E   2-7
5</td><td>SE   1-6
6</td></tr>
<tr><td>N   4-9
3</td><td>9-5
7</td><td>S   5-1
2</td></tr>
<tr><td>NW 8-4
8</td><td>W   7-3
9</td><td>SW 3-8
4</td></tr>
</table>

Sits East 2 or 3

<table>
<tr><td colspan="3" align="center">∧</td></tr>
<tr><td>SW 8-3
4</td><td>W   3-7
9</td><td>NW 4-8
8</td></tr>
<tr><td>S   1-5
2</td><td>5-9
7</td><td>N   9-4
3</td></tr>
<tr><td>SE   6-1
6</td><td>E   7-2
5</td><td>NE 2-6
1</td></tr>
</table>

Sits NW 1

<table>
<tr><td colspan="3" align="center">∧</td></tr>
<tr><td>E   1-8
5</td><td>SE   9-7
6</td><td>S   4-2
2</td></tr>
<tr><td>NE 5-3
1</td><td>8-6
7</td><td>SW 2-9
4</td></tr>
<tr><td>N   3-1
3</td><td>NW 7-5
8</td><td>W   6-4
9</td></tr>
</table>

Sits SE 1

<table>
<tr><td colspan="3" align="center">∧</td></tr>
<tr><td>W   4-6
9</td><td>NW 5-7
8</td><td>N   1-3
3</td></tr>
<tr><td>SW 9-2
4</td><td>6-8
7</td><td>NE 3-5
1</td></tr>
<tr><td>S   2-4
2</td><td>SE   7-9
6</td><td>E   8-1
5</td></tr>
</table>

Period 8
Sits SW 1

∧

N 9-6	NE 2-8	E 7-4
4	2	6
NW 4-1	5-2	SE 6-3
9	8	7
W 3-9	SW 8-5	S 1-7
1	5	3

Sits NE 1

∧

S 7-1	SW 5-8	W 9-3
3	5	1
SE 3-6	2-5	NW 1-4
7	8	9
E 4-7	NE 8-2	N 6-9
6	2	4

Sits SE 2 or 3

∧

W 5-7	NW 6-8	N 2-4
1	9	4
SW 1-3	7-9	NE 4-6
5	8	2
S 3-5	SE 8-1	E 9-2
3	7	6

Sits NW 2 or 3

∧

E 2-9	SE 1-8	S 5-3
6	7	3
NE 6-4	9-7	SW 3-1
2	8	5
N 4-2	NW 8-6	W 7-5
4	9	1

Period 9
There are no Wang Shan Wang Shui House Types in Period 9

THE DOUBLE SITTING HOUSE: ALSO KNOWN AS SHANG SHAN

"Shang Shan" translates: "The water has gone up the mountain (which it is not supposed to do)." This house type is considered inherently strong for people (health and relationships) but not as supportive for money luck. In order to balance it out and make it better for the occupants' financial luck, this house type needs water *behind* it. Having a large fountain, pool, or pond behind this house type can make it supportive for financial luck.

It will always need water behind it; the more, the better, usually. A pool can totally fix a house. A birdbath, however, will do almost nothing.

FIGURE 4B shows a house with a pool behind it.

Sometimes the Double Sitting House Type can be so good for people that a financial boost will result as a by-product. In other words, someone should not feel that a Double Sitting House cannot be good for money luck also. If a business is Double Sitting and relies on customers feeling good while at the location, it may be able to create a good enough feeling for the customers to want to return. This might easily apply to a hotel, spa, restaurant, or doctor's office, just to name a few. If the Wang Shan Wang Shui house could be labeled "A+," then the Double Sitting House could easily be "B+."

How do you recognize a Double Sitting House in the charts? If the sitting palace contains *both* Mountain and Water Stars that match the Period Star of the house, then you have a Double Sitting House. For example, a 7-7 at the sitting sector of a Period 7 house is a Double Sitting House or 4-4 at the sitting sector of a Period 4 house reveals it to be Double Sitting also.

CHARTS FOR THE DOUBLE SITTING HOUSE TYPES

Period 1
Sits South 2 or 3

∧

NW 4-7 2	N 9-2 6	NE 2-9 4
W 3-8 3	5-6 1	E 7-4 · 8
SW 8-3 7	S 1-1 5	SE 6-5 9

Sits NE 1

∧

S 9-2 5	SW 7-4 7	W 2-9 3
SE 5-6 9	4-7 1	NW 3-8 2
E 6-5 8	NE 1-1 4	N 8-3 6

Sits SW 2 or 3

∧

N 2-9 6	NE 4-7 4	E 9-2 8
NW 6-5 2	7-4 1	SE 8-3 9
W 5-6 3	SW 1-1 7	S 3-8 5

Sits East 1

∧

SW 2-9 7	W 6-5 3	NW 7-4 2
S 4-7 5	8-3 1	N 3-8 6
SE 9-2 9	E 1-1 8	NE 5-6 4

Sits West 2 or 3

∧

NE 9-2 4	E 5-6 8	SE 4-7 9
N 7-4 6	3-8 1	S 8-3 5
NW 2-9 2	W 1-1 3	SW 6-5 7

Sits NW 1

∧

E 4-7 8	SE 3-8 9	S 7-4 5
NE 8-3 4	2-9 1	SW 5-6 7
N 6-5 6	NW 1-1 2	W 9-2 3

Sits SE 2 or 3

∧

W 7-4 3	NW 8-3 2	N 4-7 6
SW 3-8 7	9-2 1	NE 6-5 4
S 5-6 5	SE 1-1 9	E 2-9 8

Sits North 1

∧

SE 7-4 9	S 2-9 5	SW 9-2 7
E 8-3 8	6-5 1	W 4-7 3
NE 3-8 4	N 1-1 6	NW 5-6 2

Period 2

Sits North 2 or 3

∧

SE 8-5 1	S 3-1 6	SW 1-3 8
E 9-4 9	7-6 2	W 5-8 4
NE 4-9 5	N 2-2 7	NW 6-7 3

Sits West 1

∧

NE 1-3 5	E 6-7 9	SE 5-8 1
N 8-5 7	4-9 2	S 9-4 6
NW 3-1 3	W 2-2 4	SW 7-6 8

Sits East 2 or 3

∧

SW 3-1 8	W 7-6 4	NW 8-5 3
S 5-8 6	9-4 2	N 4-9 7
SE 1-3 1	E 2-2 9	NE 6-7 5

Sits South 1

∧

NW 5-8 3	N 1-3 7	NE 3-1 5
W 4-9 4	6-7 2	E 8-5 9
SW 9-4 8	S 2-2 6	SE 7-6 1

Period 3
Sits NE 1

∧		
S 2-4 7	SW 9-6 9	W 4-2 5
SE 7-8 2	6-9 3	NW 5-1 4
E 8-7 1	NE 3-3 6	N 1-5 8

Sits South 2 or 3

∧		
NW 6-9 4	N 2-4 8	NE 4-2 6
W 5-1 5	7-8 3	E 9-6 1
SW 1-5 9	S 3-3 7	SE 8-7 2

Sits SW 2 or 3

∧		
N 4-2 8	NE 6-9 6	E 2-4 1
NW 8-7 4	9-6 3	SE 1-5 2
W 7-8 5	SW 3-3 9	S 5-1 7

Sits North 1

∧		
SE 9-6 2	S 4-2 7	SW 2-4 9
E 1-5 1	8-7 3	W 6-9 5
NE 5-1 6	N 3-3 8	NW 7-8 4

Period 4
Sits North 2 or 3

∧

SE 1-7	S 5-3	SW 3-5
3	8	1
E 2-6	9-8	W 7-1
2	4	6
NE 6-2	N 4-4	NW 8-9
7	9	5

Sits NW 1

∧

E 7-1	SE 6-2	S 1-7
2	3	8
NE 2-6	5-3	SW 8-9
7	4	1
N 9-8	NW 4-4	W 3-5
9	5	6

Sits SE 2 or 3

∧

W 1-7	NW 2-6	N 7-1
6	5	9
SW 6-2	3-5	NE 9-8
1	4	7
S 8-9	SE 4-4	E 5-3
8	3	2

Sits South 1

∧

NW 7-1	N 3-5	NE 5-3
5	9	7
W 6-2	8-9	E 1-7
6	4	2
SW 2-6	S 4-4	SE 9-8
1	8	3

Period 5
There are no Double Sitting House Types in Period 5

Period 6
Sits South 2 or 3

∧

NW 9-3 7	N 5-7 2	NE 7-5 9
W 8-4 8	1-2 6	E 3-9 4
SW 4-8 3	S 6-6 1	SE 2-1 5

Sits SE 1

∧

W 3-9 8	NW 4-8 7	N 9-3 2
SW 8-4 3	5-7 6	NE 2-1 9
S 1-2 1	SE 6-6 5	E 7-5 4

Sits NW 2 or 3

∧

E 9-3 4	SE 8-4 5	N 3-9 1
NE 4-8 9	7-5 6	SW 1-2 3
N 2-1 2	NW 6-6 7	W 5-7 8

Sits North 1

∧

SE 3-9 5	S 7-5 1	SW 5-7 3
E 4-8 4	2-1 6	W 9-3 8
NE 8-4 9	N 6-6 2	NW 1-2 7

Period 7
Sits SW 1

∧

N 8-6 3	NE 1-4 1	E 6-8 5
NW 3-2 8	4-1 7	SE 5-9 6
W 2-3 9	SW 7-7 4	S 9-5 2

Sits North 2 or 3

∧

SE 4-1 6	S 8-6 2	SW 6-8 4
E 5-9 5	3-2 7	W 1-4 9
NE 9-5 1	N 7-7 3	NW 2-3 8

Sits NE 2 or 3

∧

S 6-8 2	SW 4-1 4	W 8-6 9
SE 2-3 6	1-4 7	NW 9-5 8
E 3-2 5	NE 7-7 1	N 5-9 3

Sits South 1

∧

NW 1-4 8	N 6-8 3	NE 8-6 1
NW 9-5 9	2-3 7	E 4-1 5
SW 5-9 4	S 7-7 2	SE 3-2 6

Period 8
Sits South 2 or 3

^

NW 2-5 9	N 7-9 4	NE 9-7 2
W 1-6 1	3-4 8	E 5-2 6
SW 6-1 5	S 8-8 3	SE 4-3 7

Sits East 1

^

SW 9-7 5	W 4-3 1	NW 5-2 9
S 2-5 3	6-1 8	N 1-6 4
SE 7-9 7	E 8-8 6	NE 3-4 2

Sits West 2 or 3

^

NE 7-9 2	E 3-4 6	SE 2-5 7
N 5-2 4	1-6 8	S 6-1 3
NW 9-7 9	W 8-8 1	SW 4-3 5

Sits North 1

^

SE 5-2 7	S 9-7 3	SW 7-9 5
E 6-1 6	4-3 8	W 2-5 1
NE 1-6 2	N 8-8 4	NW 3-4 9

Period 9

Sits North 2 or 3

∧

SE 6-3 8	S 1-8 4	SW 8-1 6
E 7-2 7	5-4 9	W 3-6 2
NE 2-7 3	N **9-9** 5	NW 4-5 1

Sits SW 1

∧

N 1-8 5	NE 3-6 3	E 8-1 7
NW 5-4 1	6-3 9	SE 7-2 8
W 4-5 2	SW **9-9** 6	S 2-7 4

Sits NE 2 or 3

∧

S 8-1 4	SW 6-3 6	W 1-8 2
SE 4-5 8	3-6 9	NW 2-7 1
E 5-4 7	NE **9-9** 3	N 7-2 5

Sits West 1

∧

NE 8-1 3	E 4-5 7	SE 3-6 8
N 6-3 5	2-7 9	S 7-2 4
NW 1-8 1	W **9-9** 2	SW 5-4 6

Sits East 2 or 3

∧

SW 1-8	W 5-4	NW 6-3
6	2	1
S 3-6	7-2	N 2-7
4	9	5
SE 8-1	E **9-9**	NE 4-5
8	7	3

Sits SE 1

∧

W 6-3	NW 7-2	N 3-6
2	1	5
SW 2-7	8-1	NE 5-4
6	9	3
S 4-5	SE **9-9**	E 1-8
4	8	7

Sits NW 2 or 3

∧

E 3-6	SE 2-7	S 6-3
7	8	4
NE 7-2	1-8	SW 4-5
3	9	6
N 5-4	NW **9-9**	W 8-1
5	1	2

Sits South 1

∧

NW 3-6	N 8-1	NE 1-8
1	5	3
W 2-7	4-5	E 6-3
2	9	7
SW 7-2	S **9-9**	SE 5-4
6	4	8

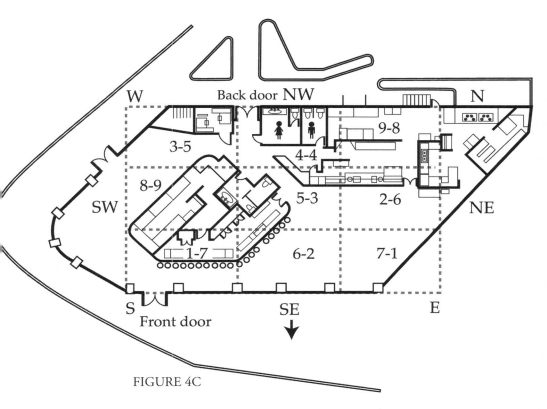

FIGURE 4C

In the restaurant floor plan shown in Fig. 4C you can see there is a front entrance located in the 1-7 sector. This is good for business, including a restaurant with a bar since the 1-7 energies encourage drinking. The 1-7 Stars can encourage people to eat and drink and feed addictive behaviors. The 1 Star is associated with alcohol, and the bar is right in this zone. The 7 (Dui) Star is also related to the mouth. The back door brings people in through the 4-4 sector. This is a heavily used door because it is right near a major parking structure for the area. The 4-4 energy attracts creative people. This restaurant is almost across the street from Sony Studios. The 4 Star is also associated with "romance" energy, so it is the kind of restaurant that will attract people looking to meet someone or to go on a date.

The restaurant also contains a bakery and deli, and when you study the floor plan, it couldn't get any better than to have a kitchen and the cash register in the 8-9 and 9-8 areas. The product (food) is made in the major prosperity zones, and the money is collected there, too. This is an example of a floor plan that utilizes all the best Feng Shui energies for maximum potential and to appeal to the very type of patrons the restaurant wishes to attract. It is also an example of how a Double Sitting chart can be very good for money.

THE DOUBLE FACING HOUSE: ALSO KNOWN AS XIA SHUI

"Xia Shui" translates: "The Mountain Star has gone down to the water." The Double Facing House is considered inherently strong for money luck but not as good for supporting health and relationships. The occupants could do well financially, but the marriage might suffer, or the occupants could make a lot of money, but their health might become compromised. This house type needs a mountain on the facing side to fix it. As mentioned earlier, a building across the street can work

FIGURE 4D. The illustration in Fig. 4D shows a single-story house with a two-story house across the street, acting as a mountain.

as a mountain type of energy if it is taller than the Double Facing House. Other ways to create a mountain include having an elevated landscape on the facing side or by bringing in stone statues for the facing side.

Really tall trees that are taller than the house can assume the role of a mountain, but generally it is best to have something earthen that is at least a few feet high on the facing side. I have instructed clients to create an elevated flowerbed, some brick work, even a half-stone wall. For a wall to work as a mountain remedy, it cannot be attached to the house. The wall must only be in front of the house, not attached to its sides.

On a practical level, this might seem to defeat the point of having a wall to begin with, if it is not attached to the house. I would say that if the wall stretches across the front of the house and even on the sides but is connected to the house with a wooden gate, then that would qualify as an unattached mountain. A stone façade to a house would not qualify as a mountain in front of the house. Sometimes the mountain energy occurs naturally and inconspicuously, such as the house where there is a brick pillar for a mailbox or a series of brick light posts in front of the house. Whatever you decide upon for mountain energy in front of the house, it should look nice.

FIGURE 4E shows a brick wall in front of a house acting as a mountain.

FIGURE 4F. The illustration in Fig. 4F is of an elevated flowerbed in front of a house.

The Double Facing House does not really need water in front of it to fix any problems, but water in front can enhance it further for money luck. So, I can see an opportunity for a large stone fountain or waterfall on the facing side of the Double Facing House, combining both water and mountain remedies. You can see this more often in front of a commercial structure. To be clear, it is the mountain that is needed on the facing side of the Double Facing House, and water can be thrown in for extra credit. In the same way, the Double Sitting House really needs water *behind* it, but if there is a mountain and water combination, that is fine, too. How do you recognize the chart for the Double Facing House? After charting out the whole luo shu grid, if the facing palace has a set of numbers (both Mountain and Water Stars) that mimics the Period Star of the house, then it is Double Facing. An example would be 3-3 in the facing palace of a Period 3 house or 8-8 in the facing palace of a Period 8 house.

CHARTS FOR THE DOUBLE FACING HOUSE TYPES

Period 1

Sits SW 1

∧

N 3-8 6	NE **1-1** 4	E 5-6 8
NW 8-3 2	7-4 1	SE 6-5 9
W 9-2 3	SW 4-7 7	S 2-9 5

Sits NE 2 or 3

∧

S 8-3 5	SW **1-1** 7	W 6-5 3
SE 3-8 9	4-7 1	NW 5-6 2
E 2-9 8	NE 7-4 4	N 9-2 6

Sits North 2 or 3

∧

SE 5-6 9	S **1-1** 5	SW 3-8 7
E 4-7 8	6-5 1	W 8-3 3
NE 9-2 4	N 2-9 6	NW 7-4 2

Sits West 1

∧

NE 6-5 4	E **1-1** 8	SE 2-9 9
N 8-3 6	3-8 1	S 7-4 5
NW 4-7 2	W 5-6 3	SW 9-2 7

Sits East 2 or 3

∧

SW 5-6	W 1-1	NW 9-2
7	3	2
S 3-8	8-3	N 4-7
5	1	6
SE 7-4	E 6-5	NE 2-9
9	8	4

Sits SE 1

∧

W 2-9	NW 1-1	N 5-6
3	2	6
SW 6-5	9-2	NE 3-8
7	1	4
S 4-7	SE 8-3	E 7-4
5	9	8

Sits NW 2 or 3

∧

E 9-2	SE 1-1	S 6-5
8	9	5
NE 5-6	2-9	SW 8-3
4	1	7
N 7-4	NW 3-8	W 4-7
6	2	3

Sits South 1

∧

NW 6-5	N 1-1	NE 8-3
2	6	4
W 7-4	5-6	E 3-8
3	1	8
SW 2-9	S 9-2	SE 4-7
7	5	9

Period 2
Sits South 2 or 3

∧

NW 7-6 3	N 2-2 7	NE 9-4 5
W 8-5 4	6-7 2	E 4-9 9
SW 3-1 8	S 1-3 6	SE 5-8 1

Sits East 1

∧

SW 6-7 8	W 2-2 4	NW 1-3 3
S 4-9 6	9-4 2	N 5-8 7
SE 8-5 1	E 7-6 9	NE 3-1 5

Sits West 2 or 3

∧

NE 7-6 5	E 2-2 9	SE 3-1 1
N 9-4 7	4-9 2	S 8-5 6
NW 5-8 3	W 6-7 4	SW 1-3 8

Sits North 1

∧

SE 6-7 1	S 2-2 6	SW 4-9 8
E 5-8 9	7-6 2	W 9-4 4
NE 1-3 5	N 3-1 7	NW 8-5 3

Period 3
Sits North 2 or 3

∧

SE 7-8 2	S 3-3 7	SW 5-1 9
E 6-9 1	8-7 3	W 1-5 5
NE 2-4 6	N 4-2 8	NW 9-6 4

Sits SW 1

∧

N 5-1 8	NE 3-3 6	SE 7-8 1
NW 1-5 4	9-6 3	SE 8-7 2
W 2-4 5	SW 6-9 9	S 4-2 7

Sits NE 2 or 3

∧

S 1-5 7	SW 3-3 9	W 8-7 5
SE 5-1 2	6-9 3	NW 7-8 4
E 4-2 1	NE 9-6 6	N 2-4 8

Sits South 1

∧

NW 8-7 4	N 3-3 8	NE 1-5 6
W 9-6 5	7-8 3	E 5-1 1
SW 4-2 9	S 2-4 7	SE 6-9 2

Period 4
Sits South 2 or 3

^

NW 9-8	N 4-4	NE 2-6
5	9	7
W 1-7	8-9	E 6-2
6	4	2
SW 5-3	S 3-5	SE 7-1
1	8	3

Sits SE 1

^

W 5-3	NW 4-4	N 8-9
6	5	9
SW 9-8	3-5	NE 6-2
1	4	7
S 7-1	SE 2-6	E 1-7
8	3	2

Sits NW 2 or 3

^

E 3-5	SE 4-4	S 9-8
2	3	8
NE 8-9	5-3	SW 2-6
7	4	1
N 1-7	NW 6-2	W 7-1
9	5	6

Sits North 1

^

SE 8-9	S 4-4	SW 6-2
3	8	1
E 7-1	9-8	W 2-6
2	4	6
NE 3-5	N 5-3	NW 1-7
7	9	5

Period 5
There are no Double Facing House Types in Period 5

Period 6
Sits North 2 or 3

∧

SE 1-2	S 6-6	SW 8-4
5	1	3
E 9-3	2-1	W 4-8
4	6	8
NE 5-7	N 7-5	NW 3-9
9	2	7

Sits NW 1

∧

E 5-7	SE 6-6	S 2-1
4	5	1
NE 1-2	7-5	SW 4-8
9	6	3
N 3-9	NW 8-4	W 9-3
2	7	8

Sits SE 2 or 3

∧

W 7-5	NW 6-6	N 1-2
8	7	2
SW 2-1	5-7	NE 8-4
3	6	9
S 9-3	SE 4-8	E 3-9
1	5	4

Sits South 1

∧

NW 2-1	N 6-6	NE 4-8
7	2	9
W 3-9	1-2	E 8-4
8	6	4
SW 7-5	S 5-7	SE 9-3
3	1	5

Period 7

Sits South 2 or 3

^

NW 3-2	N 7-7	NE 5-9
8	3	1
W 4-1	2-3	E 9-5
9	7	5
SW 8-6	S 6-8	SE 1-4
4	2	6

Sits NE 1

^

S 5-9	SW 7-7	W 3-2
2	4	9
SE 9-5	1-4	NW 2-3
6	7	8
E 8-6	NE 4-1	N 6-8
5	1	3

Sits SW 2 or 3

^

N 9-5	NE 7-7	E 2-3
3	1	5
NW 5-9	4-1	SE 3-2
8	7	6
W 6-8	SW 1-4	S 8-6
9	4	2

Sits North 1

^

SE 2-3	S 7-7	SW 9-5
6	2	4
E 1-4	3-2	W 5-9
5	7	9
NE 6-8	N 8-6	NW 4-1
1	3	8

Period 8
Sits North 2 or 3

∧

SE 3-4	S 8-8	SW 1-6
7	3	5
E 2-5	4-3	W 6-1
6	8	1
NE 7-9	N 9-7	NW 5-2
2	4	9

Sits West 1

∧

NE 4-3	E 8-8	SE 9-7
2	6	7
N 6-1	1-6	S 5-2
4	8	3
NW 2-5	W 3-4	SW 7-9
9	1	5

Sits East 2 or 3

∧

SW 3-4	W 8-8	NW 7-9
5	1	9
S 1-6	6-1	N 2-5
3	8	4
SE 5-2	E 4-3	NE 9-7
7	6	2

Sits South 1

∧

NW 4-3	N 8-8	NE 6-1
9	4	2
W 5-2	3-4	E 1-6
1	8	6
SW 9-7	S 7-9	SE 2-5
5	3	7

Period 9

Sits South 2 or 3

∧

NW 5-4 1	N 9-9 5	NE 7-2 3
W 6-3 2	4-5 9	E 2-7 7
SW 1-8 6	S 8-1 4	SE 3-6 8

Sits NE 1

∧

S 7-2 4	SW 9-9 6	W 5-4 2
SE 2-7 8	3-6 9	NW 4-5 1
E 1-8 7	NE 6-3 3	N 8-1 5

Sits SW 2 or 3

∧

N 2-7 5	NE 9-9 3	E 4-5 7
NW 7-2 1	6-3 9	SE 5-4 8
W 8-1 2	SW 3-6 6	S 1-8 4

Sits East 1

∧

SW 4-5 6	W 9-9 2	NW 8-1 1
S 2-7 4	7-2 9	N 3-6 5
SE 6-3 8	E 5-4 7	NE 1-8 3

Sits West 2 or 3

⋀

NE 5-4 3	E 9-9 7	SE 1-8 8
N 7-2 5	2-7 9	S 6-3 4
NW 3-6 1	W 4-5 2	SW 8-1 6

Sits NW 1

⋀

E 8-1 7	SE 9-9 8	S 5-4 4
NE 4-5 3	1-8 9	SW 7-2 6
N 6-3 5	NW 2-7 1	W 3-6 2

Sits SE 2 or 3

⋀

W 1-8 2	NW 9-9 1	N 4-5 5
SW 5-4 6	8-1 9	NE 2-7 3
S 3-6 4	SE 7-2 8	E 6-3 7

Sits North 1

⋀

SE 4-5 8	S 9-9 4	SW 2-7 6
E 3-6 7	5-4 9	W 7-2 2
NE 8-1 3	N 1-8 5	NW 6-3 1

THE REVERSED HOUSE: ALSO KNOWN AS SHANG SHAN XIA SHUI

The Reversed House is the exact opposite of the Wang Shan Wang Shui house. There is a tendency for this house to undermine both the health and financial luck of the occupants. The Reversed House needs water behind it to make it better for money luck and a mountain in front of it to make it better for people luck. This is one example of how advanced Flying Star Feng Shui is so much more specific and accurate than the more simple Form School methods. For instance, in many Form School books, there is a description of the ideal house having a mountain behind it for protection, like a back support, and a lovely stream passing before it on the facing side. This might be true for the Wang Shan Wang Shui house, but not for the Reversed House. It needs the exact opposite features in the outside environment.

Of all the Feng Shui remedies I have seen work for people over many years of consulting, placing water *behind* a Reversed House has

FIGURE 4G shows a house with a fountain behind it and a big mountain in front of it.

clearly been one of the most helpful. In fact, Reversed Houses might suffer an unnecessarily bad reputation, considering that they can be relatively easy to fix. And who wouldn't enjoy a nice water feature in the backyard? In fact, I really prefer having a water feature in the back to a fountain at the front of the house, where you only see it when you are coming and going.

Classifying a house as being bad for money is also tricky because wealth is such a relative experience and state of consciousness. I have had many clients who lived in Reversed Houses and seemed to be doing great financially. We can argue that they would do even better if they were living in a Wang Shan Wang Shui house, but this is an example of where personal destiny might override or mitigate less-than-perfect Feng Shui. In other words, the Reversed House is not an automatic recipe for failure.

In *The Feng Shui Matrix*, I outlined how we have other major influences in our lives, with destiny coming first, then luck (as in the Chinese Luck Pillars), third is Feng Shui, and then comes spiritual practices and beliefs. As well, there are other influences upon us that we may never know about. There is a branch of astrology called Astro-cartography, which maps out the best places on the planet for someone to live. It is really like "big picture" Feng Shui because our goal is to be in harmony with our environment. Astro-cartography may be an extension of that. In other words, if living in California is not good for you but living in Texas is, then whatever Feng Shui you encounter in a certain city or place might take a back seat to what part of the country or world you live in. I do know of individuals who always felt blocked living in a certain city, but as soon as they moved to another area, their lives did flow much more smoothly. This is just one example of how many other influences can be taken into consideration.

Lastly, if I did not believe in the distinctions between the four major house types, I would not have categorized them into these divisions. But it also troubles me when beginning Feng Shui students go into a complete panic when they discover they are living in a Reversed House type. There is so much more to Feng Shui than these four basic house types that they should never be taken as the one ruling or defining aspect to grade the house.

How do you recognize a Reversed House Flying Star chart? You have to take note of the positioning of the Mountain Star and the Water Star in each of the sitting and facing palaces. If the Period Star for the house lands in the Water Star position in the sitting palace and the Period number lands in the Mountain Star position in the facing palace, then you have a Reversed House. An example of this would be a Period 6 house with a 6-9 in the facing and a 3-6 in the sitting. The 6 Stars are essentially in the wrong location. They are "reversed" from what they should be. An apartment or a commercial building that is a Reversed Type could be at a significant disadvantage since one has little or no control over the exteriors. But sometimes, as luck would have it, there can be a correction in place. I have seen apartments that were Reversed Type, but the building's community pool might have been positioned behind the client's apartment, working just as well as a pool behind a private house. One more thing I'd like to mention to help lessen the stigma of the Reversed House is that they are extremely common. For example, in the San Fernando Valley section of Los Angeles County where I frequently go to consult, the vast majority of Period 5 houses are Reversed Houses! Many thousands of them are Reversed Type! And the world over, there are millions, of course.

Within my own area of influence I have seen with great consistency that the people who have pools behind their Reversed Houses do much better financially than those who do not. And that should be a major point: Thousands of gallons of water can correct a problem, but a pitifully small fountain or birdbath outside will do almost nothing to improve the house type. In warm climates, people can maintain water features outside all the time whereas in some parts of the country and world winter would freeze an outside fountain. Some people just need to forgo their outside remedies during freezing weather. I do, however, have a few clients who keep their fountains flowing even in snow by using special warming devices for their fountains or Koi ponds. That's dedication!

CHARTS FOR THE REVERSED HOUSE TYPES

Period 1
There are no Reversed House Types in Period 1

Period 2
Sits SW 2 or 3

∧

N	4-1 7	NE	2-8 5	E	6-3 9
NW	9-6 3		8-5 2	SE	7-4 1
W	1-7 4	SW	5-2 8	S	3-9 6

Sits NE 2 or 3

∧

S	9-3 6	SW	2-5 8	W	7-1 4
SE	4-7 1		5-8 2	NW	6-9 3
E	3-6 9	NE	8-2 5	N	1-4 7

Sits NW 1

∧

E	1-8 9	SE	2-9 1	S	7-5 6
NE	6-4 5		3-1 2	SW	9-7 8
N	8-6 7	NW	4-2 3	W	5-3 4

Sits SE 1

∧

W	3-5 4	NW	2-4 3	N	6-8 7
SW	7-9 8		1-3 2	NE	4-6 5
S	5-7 6	SE	9-2 1	E	8-1 9

Period 3
Sits West 1

∧

NE 8-4 6	E 3-8 1	SE 4-9 2
N 1-6 8	5-1 3	S 9-5 7
NW 6-2 4	W 7-3 5	SW 2-7 9

Sits East 1

∧

SW 7-2 9	W 3-7 5	NW 2-6 4
S 5-9 7	1-5 3	N 6-1 8
SE 9-4 2	E 8-3 1	NE 4-8 6

Sits SE 2 or 3

∧

W 4-6 5	NW 3-5 4	N 7-9 8
SW 8-1 9	2-4 3	NE 5-7 6
S 6-8 7	SE 1-3 2	E 9-2 1

Sits NW 2 or 3

∧

E 2-9 1	SE 3-1 2	S 8-6 7
NE 7-5 6	4-2 3	SW 1-8 9
N 9-7 8	NW 5-3 4	W 6-4 5

Period 4
Sits SW 1

∧

N 6-3	NE 4-1	E 8-5
9	7	2
NW 2-8	1-7	SE 9-6
5	4	3
W 3-9	SW 7-4	S 5-2
6	1	8

Sits NE 1

∧

S 2-5	SW 4-7	W 9-3
8	1	6
SE 6-9	7-1	NW 8-2
3	4	5
E 5-8	NE 1-4	N 3-6
2	7	9

Sits West 2 or 3

∧

NE 5-9	E 9-4	SE 1-5
7	2	3
N 7-2	2-6	S 6-1
9	4	8
NW 3-7	W 4-8	SW 8-3
5	6	1

Sits East 2 or 3

∧

SW 8-3	W 4-8	NW 3-7
1	6	5
S 6-1	2-6	N 7-2
8	4	9
SE 1-5	E 9-4	NE 5-9
3	2	7

Period 5

Sits SW 2 or 3

∧

N 7-4	NE 5-2	E 9-6
1	8	3
NW 3-9	2-8	SE 1-7
6	5	4
W 4-1	SW 8-5	S 6-3
7	2	9

Sits NE 2 or 3

∧

S 3-6	SW 5-8	W 1-4
9	2	7
SE 7-1	8-2	NW 9-3
4	5	6
E 6-9	NE 2-5	N 4-7
3	8	1

Sits West 1

∧

NE 1-6	E 5-1	SE 6-2
8	3	4
N 3-8	7-3	S 2-7
1	5	9
NW 8-4	W 9-5	SW 4-9
6	7	2

Sits East 1

∧

SW 9-4	W 5-9	NW 4-8
2	7	6
S 7-2	3-7	N 8-3
9	5	1
SE 2-6	E 1-5	NE 6-1
4	3	8

Sits SE 2 or 3

∧

W 6-8 7	NW 5-7 6	N 9-2 1
SW 1-3 2	4-6 5	NE 7-9 8
S 8-1 9	SE 3-5 4	E 2-4 3

Sits NW 2 or 3

∧

E 4-2 3	SE 5-3 4	S 1-8 9
NE 9-7 8	6-4 5	SW 3-1 2
N 2-9 1	NW 7-5 6	W 8-6 7

Sits North 1

∧

SE 9-8 4	S 5-4 9	SW 7-6 2
E 8-7 3	1-9 5	W 3-2 7
NE 4-3 8	N 6-5 1	NW 2-1 6

Sits South 1

∧

NW 1-2 6	N 5-6 1	NE 3-4 8
W 2-3 7	9-1 5	E 7-8 3
SW 6-7 2	S 4-5 9	SE 8-9 4

Period 6
Sits SW 1

∧

N 8-5	NE **6-3**	E 1-7
2	9	4
NW 4-1	3-9	SE 2-8
7	6	5
W 5-2	SW **9-6**	S 7-4
8	3	1

Sits NE 1

∧

S 4-7	SW **6-9**	W 2-5
1	3	8
SE 8-2	9-3	NW 1-4
5	6	7
E 7-1	NE 3-**6**	N 5-8
4	9	2

Sits West 2 or 3

∧

NE 2-7	E **6-2**	SE 7-3
9	4	5
N 4-9	8-4	S 3-8
2	6	1
NW 9-5	W **1-6**	SW 5-1
7	8	3

Sits East 2 or 3

∧

SW 1-5	W **6-1**	NW 5-9
3	8	7
S 8-3	4-8	N 9-4
1	6	2
SE 3-7	E **2-6**	NE 7-2
5	4	9

Period 7
Sits West 1

∧

NE 3-8 1	E 7-3 5	SE 8-4 6
N 5-1 3	9-5 7	S 4-9 2
NW 1-6 8	W 2-7 9	SW 6-2 4

Sits East 1

∧

SW 2-6 4	W 7-2 9	NW 6-1 8
S 9-4 2	5-9 7	N 1-5 3
SE 4-8 6	E 3-7 5	NE 8-3 1

Sits SE 2 or 3

∧

W 8-1 9	NW 7-9 8	N 2-4 3
SW 3-5 4	6-8 7	NE 9-2 1
S 1-3 2	SE 5-7 6	E 4-6 5

Sits NW 2 or 3

∧

E 6-4 5	SE 7-5 6	S 3-1 2
NE 2-9 1	8-6 7	SW 5-3 4
N 4-2 3	NW 9-7 8	W 1-8 9

Period 8

Sits SW 2 or 3

∧

N 1-7	NE **8-5**	E 3-9
4	2	6
NW 6-3	5-2	SE 4-1
9	8	7
W 7-4	SW **2-8**	S 9-6
1	5	3

Sits NE 2 or 3

∧

S 6-9	SW **8-2**	W 4-7
3	5	1
SE 1-4	2-5	NW 3-6
7	8	9
E 9-3	NE **5-8**	N 7-1
6	2	4

Sits NW 1

∧

E 7-5	SE **8-6**	S 4-2
6	7	3
NE 3-1	9-7	SW 6-4
2	8	5
N 5-3	NW 1-**8**	W 2-9
4	9	1

Sits SE 1

∧

W 9-2	NW **8-1**	N 3-5
1	9	4
SW 4-6	7-9	NE 1-3
5	8	2
S 2-4	SE **6-8**	E 5-7
3	7	6

Period 9
There are no Reversed House Types in Period 9

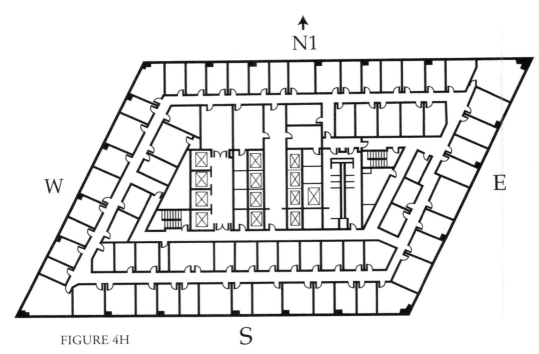

FIGURE 4H

The shape of this building in Fig. 4H has an auspicious feature that was probably designed without any Feng Shui knowledge. It was built in Period 7, and it faces North 1. The individual offices on each floor that face North 1 are Double Sitting offices. The South-facing offices are Double Facing. Because of the angle of the sides, both the East 2 and West 2 offices end up being Wang Shan Wang Shui. Had this office been built with parallel sides instead of the angle, the East and West offices would have been the Reversed Type.

THE ENDURING NATURE OF
THE FOUR MAJOR HOUSE TYPES

Some schools teach that the four basic house types can relinquish their titles once the house goes beyond its original Construction Period. This would mean a Reversed House built in Period 7 might not have the influence of being a Reversed Type once Period 8 starts. I do think the status might fade a bit but not change entirely. I think the four basic house types can have an enduring effect beyond the first twenty years after the houses have been built. This might be the same as people maintaining the same basic personality throughout their lives but mellowing with age. With the four major house types comes a prescription for adding water and mountain forms to either the facing or sitting side. Different schools of Feng Shui will disagree about whether those forms should be maintained once the house outlasts its own Construction Period.

There is also a generally supported theory that the Double Sitting and Reversed House types should have water placed behind them exactly aligned with the sitting palace of the house (and not deviate to a side area in the back) in order to be most effective. But in some schools of Feng Shui, the idea of putting water close to an "untimely" star could cause more negatives than positives, even if the original intent was to "un-reverse" the house.

There are also more advanced "Water Dragon Formulae," which suggest that water features could be placed in other locations around a property that have nothing to do with when the house was built but are based more on the current era. In *The Feng Shui Matrix* I highlight the two most powerful areas to place outside water in any given twenty-year era, as well as where to avoid placing outside water in any given twenty-year era.

Although I have been practicing Feng Shui a good amount of time, even spanning through Periods 7 and 8 is not long enough to collect sufficient case studies on the changing nature of the four major house types. Sometimes the remedies might work in one way that makes it impossible to verify whether something else is beneficial as well. For example, I have evaluated many Reversed Period 5 houses and found that adding water behind them helped the occupants improve their finances. This would suggest that the house types *maintain* their original nature even beyond their Construction Era. But with many of those houses, I suggested water behind the properties to the East or Southwest since those have been two key areas for outside water placement since 1984 and will continue to be so until 2024. So, how can I say with 100% confidence that the water was working effectively for one reason and not another or for both?

CHAPTER FIVE

Special Flying Star Charts

ANOTHER TYPE OF WANG HOUSE

The four house types provide a very sophisticated way of understanding an important feature of a house, but learning which type your house is should be the bare minimum you should expect out of a professional Feng Shui consultation. If someone claims to be a Feng Shui expert and does not even know about these four major house classifications, then this is someone who has not even learned the rudiments of classical Feng Shui.

There is another type of Wang Shan Wang Shui house that often goes unnoticed, perhaps because it becomes a Wang Shan Wang Shui directly after the Construction Period in which it was built. This feature would support the theory that a house type can change in different Periods.

Again, you will want to look at the sitting and facing palaces of its chart in order to identify it. Sometimes this house type is called Wang Shan *Sheng* Shui. The word "sheng" means "healthful and positive," and it also relates to the cycle a Flying Star is in. If a Flying Star is in a "sheng" cycle, then it is in a good phase that is going to get better during the following twenty years.

For example: A house that is built in Period 7 and sits South 1 has the 7-7 Flying Stars in the sitting palace, making it technically a Double Sitting House. But the facing palace of this house type has the 6-8 Flying Stars. Since the Flying Star 8 was in a sheng cycle during Period 7, it had a kind of "vice-presidential" aura to it of up-and-coming energy, waiting its turn to take over. Then, when Period 8 began, the Flying Star 8 for this house type was already in the correct position (Water Star position in the facing palace). The 6-8 Stars in the facing palace show the 8 Star to be the Wang number in Period 8. "Wang place, Wang time" can be a good thing! One thing that happens as a person deepens his or her Feng Shui knowledge is that he or she will first learn the rules and then the exceptions to the rules. Finally, the Feng Shui Master will know how to break the rules.

Here is an example of a Wang Shan *Sheng* Shui House Type, built in Period 8.

Sits South 2 or 3

∧

NW 2-5 9	N 7-9 4	NE 9-7 2
W 1-6 1	3-4 8	E 5-2 6
SW 6-1 5	S 8-8 3	SE 4-3 7

In the above example, the Double Sitting Period 8 House has the 9 Water Star in the facing palace, so when Period 9 begins, this house will become better for money luck, an "almost Wang Shan Wang Shui" house during Period 9.

YET ANOTHER TYPE OF WANG HOUSE

This house type is also based on timing and direction, but in a much simpler format. It is just another layer to consider. In each twenty-year era, there is a direction that is considered Wang, or especially strong.

In *The Feng Shui Matrix*, I outlined this in a formula for determining the best and worst places to have an outside water feature. It has everything to do with direction and timing. Just the sitting or facing side of a house can sometimes serve to classify it as being a little luckier in a certain Period. For example, Period 8 is associated with the Gen Trigram, the direction of Northeast. During Period 8, a house that *sits* Northeast can extract more good qi from that direction to benefit the health of the occupants. Equally, houses that *face* Northeast will be a little luckier for financial gain during Period 8. Though this is not obvious, a house receives energy from these relative directions. If a house receives Wang energy on its sitting side, then it can support health better. If the house faces the Wang direction energy, then it is a little better for financial support. *This is only true for houses that sit in sector 2 of their direction.*

A Chart for the Wang Direction House

Houses are often characterized by their sitting directions, so the "name" of the house reflects the Trigram name of that direction and is also noted in the sitting column below.

During Period	Sits: Especially Good for Health	Faces: Especially Good for Finances
1	North 2 / Kan House	North 2
2	SW 2 / Kun House	SW 2
3	East 2 / Zhen House	East 2
4	SE 2 / Xun House	SE 2
5	No House type	*No House type*
6	NW 2 / Qian House	NW 2
7	West 2 / Dui House	West 2
8	NE 2 / Gen House	NE 2
9	South 2 / Li House	South 2

This concept of direction in relation to the "Wang" direction spills over into some of the folk remedies that you may hear about. For example, knowing that Period 8 is associated with the direction of Northeast is why some Feng Shui adherents will place an elephant figurine facing Northeast in Period 8. The "trunk-up" elephant supposedly sucks in the Wang energy from the Wang direction. This is supposed to be a prosperity remedy. In Period 9, the same folk remedy would need to be placed facing South since Period 9 is associated with the South direction. This is also why some people think a lake to the South of a house will be capable of attracting "future" money luck in Period 8, since water is known to attract prosperity qi. What is future money luck? It could be seen as spiritual brownie points that you will collect in the future. An example might be a person who works hard and finds the fruits of his or her labor manifesting later rather than immediately. The more authentic Feng Shui you learn, the more you will understand where the myths, superstitions, and folk remedies come from. You will understand how genuine principles get diluted.

For example, in Chinese astrology, each year you will have a relationship with another zodiac sign that can work as a benefactor remedy for you. If the prognosis indicates having a bad year but you spend time with a person who has a certain positive zodiac sign for that year, then your prognosis gets better. That person's good energy rubs off on you. There is a real energetic connection between two people of different signs. But the diluted version of that theory is when people think they can improve their luck by wearing a pendant of that particular zodiac sign. For example, in the year 2007, people born in the Year of the Ox could have benefited from spending time with a person born in the Year of the Snake. If such a person was a family member or good friend, then it is easy to have that beneficial personal connection. But this does not mean the Ox person should have worn a Snake pendant necklace to change his or her fortune for the year. Such behavior is an example of a myth or superstition. It is also how a lot of products and trinkets get sold in the name of Feng Shui.

LOCKED PERIODS

Every house, no matter what other category it falls into, will experience periods of time known as "Locked Periods" or "Imprisoned Stars." A house can be locked for money, which undermines financial potential, or it can be locked for people, which undermines health and relationships.

The house can be in a twenty-year Lock for Money or for People, but never at the same time for both twenty-year Locks. The twenty-year Locked Periods will occur once in every 180-year complete cycle of the house. A house can be in a one-year Money Lock or People Lock, and that will repeat every nine years. A house can be in monthly or daily Locked Periods as well. Obviously, the most intense kind of Locked Period is one that lasts for twenty years. This can have long-term effects on the occupants. Annual Locked Periods can also predict when a person will have a singularly worse year for health and relationships or finances, especially if there are compounding aspects to the Feng Shui.

For example, if a house is in a twenty-year Locked Period, concurrent with a one-year Locked Period, it can be like someone serving concurrent jail sentences, a double whammy. Then, if there are other bad Flying Star combinations or uncorrected flaws, this can increase the chances for something momentous to occur.

A twenty-year Locked Period, especially at its beginning, is a negative feature to a house, which might be one of several reasons to not buy it. A long-term People Lock can undermine fertility and relationships. The number of people in a house will stay the same while the occupants are "imprisoned." So, if a single person moves into a house during a twenty-year People Lock, it will be harder for him or her to get married. If a couple moves into a house during a twenty-year People Lock, it will be harder for them to conceive a child, which is an example of bringing another human being into the house. I've seen a few exceptions where personal destiny could overrule this principle, but it has almost always involved fertility drugs.

Knowing about monthly Lock Periods can be useful when people are trying to do something where they need the monthly energy to help them. This can involve moving, starting, or finding a new job, getting pregnant, starting construction, and a whole bunch of other events or circumstances in which the monthly Lock Period can take a more important role than usual.

How to Determine Whether a House Is in a Twenty-Year Money Lock

There are several ways to figure this out mathematically, but once you have determined the Stars that are to be placed in the center palace, if the Water Star matches the current Period, then that house is currently in a twenty-year Money Lock for the duration of that Period.

See the chart below for a Period 6 East-sitting/West-facing house. The Center Stars are 4-8 with the 8 Star relating to money. You can think of it as being "trapped" in the center. So this house is in a twenty-year Money Lock from 2004–2023, i.e., the whole of Period 8.

NE	E	SE
N	4-8 6	S
NW	W	SW

V

Below is another chart for a Southeast-sitting/Northwest-facing house built in Period 7. It is in a twenty-year Money Lock for Period 8. In any given Period, there will be several house types that are in a twenty-year Money Lock. This includes houses that are normally Wang Shan Wang Shui, but, of course, it is worse for houses that are the Reversed type.

E	SE	S
NE	6-8 7	SW
N	NW	W

V

A house cannot be in a twenty-year Money Lock in the same Period in which it was built. Houses that face the Northwest, however, will always enter a twenty-year Money Lock as soon as they go into the very next Period. Other house types might not enter a twenty-year Money Lock until many decades have passed after their construction.

How to Determine Whether a House Is in a Twenty-Year People Lock

If a house is in a twenty-year People Lock, you can look to the Center Stars, note the number of the Mountain Star, and see whether it matches the current era we are in. If so, then the house is in a twenty-year People Lock. See the example below of a house that sits South and faces North and was built in Period 4. You don't even have to float all the numbers throughout the chart to determine whether the house is in a Locked Period. Just look at the Center Stars. This chart shows a house type that is in a twenty-year People Lock in Period 8, and it will also be in a twenty-year Money Lock in Period 9.

SE	S	SW
E	8-9 4	W
NE	N	NW

V

How to Determine Whether a House Is in a One-Year Money Lock

A house is in a one-year Money Lock if the Water Star in the center matches the current Annual Star in the center. Below is an example of a house, built in Period 6, sitting North and facing South. The combination of 2-1 in the center indicates that whenever there is an Annual 1 Star in the center palace this house will be in a one-year Money Lock.

There will be an Annual 1 Star in the center of all structures in the year 2008, and then the cycle repeats every nine years, including in 2017.

NW	N	NE
W	2-1 6	E
SW	S	SE

v

How to Determine Whether a House Is in a One-Year People Lock

If the house has a Mountain Star in the center palace that matches the current Annual Number in the center, then you have a one-year People Lock. You can also go back in time with any of these locked formulae and note when your house was locked in the past. Below is a chart for a house built in Period 4 that sits North and faces South. The Annual Star in the center is 9 in the year 2009. So it will match the Mountain Star 9 in the center, indicating a one-year People Lock in this house in 2009. As well, this house is concurrently in a twenty-year Money Lock in all of Period 8. So, 2009 could be a bad year for these occupants with a one-year People Lock concurrent with a twenty-year Money Lock.

NW	N	NE
W	9-8 4	E
SW	S	SE

v

The emphasis of this book is not as much on the Annual Stars as on the permanent Flying Stars of a structure, but in my first two books I go over in more detail the influences of the Annual Stars. For a quick reference, the chart below can tell you instantly where the Annual Stars are in a perpetual nine-year cycle. For the purposes of just determining a one-year Lock, you need only look at the Annual Star in the center each year. The Annual Number/Star in the center *descends* as the years move forward. Then, you *ascend* the floating of the numbers through each direction exactly the same way you do the Construction Cycle Number (Period Star).

Annual Chart

Year	2008 2017	2009 2018	2010 2019	2011 2020	2012 2021	2013 2022	2014 2023	2015 2024	2016 2025
Center	1	9	8	7	6	5	4	3	2
NW	2	1	9	8	7	6	5	4	3
W	3	2	1	9	8	7	6	5	4
NE	4	3	2	1	9	8	7	6	5
S	5	4	3	2	1	9	8	7	6
N	6	5	4	3	2	1	9	8	7
SW	7	6	5	4	3	2	1	9	8
E	8	7	6	5	4	3	2	1	9
SE	9	8	7	6	5	4	3	2	1

If you were to include the Annual Stars in your basic Flying Star chart, you would glean even more about the influences of the area and the timeliness of when certain things might happen. You can review the list of the individual Flying Stars 1 through 9 to understand how any Annual Star might behave in a certain part of the house. The Annual Stars act as triggers or stimulators to the Mountain and Water Stars.

How to Determine Whether a House Is in a Monthly Lock, for People or for Money

Determining a monthly Lock, be it for people or for money, is identical to how you find a one-year Lock. If the monthly number in the center matches the Mountain Star, you have a monthly People Lock. If the monthly number in the center matches the Water Star in the center, then you have a monthly Money Lock. These come and go quickly and should not be used as criteria for buying a house. Every single structure will go through a couple of monthly Locked periods every year.

The Monthly Number/Star in the center begins each solar year (February 4th) with an 8, 5, or 2 Star depending on the zodiac (year branch) of the Chinese year. Then, the monthly numbers will ascend through

Chart for Monthly Center Star

Month: Begins Approximately	Year of the Rat, Rabbit, Horse, Rooster	Year of the Ox, Dragon, Sheep, Dog	Year of the Tiger, Tiger, Snake, Monkey, Pig
Feb 5th	8 in the center, etc.	5 in the center, etc.	2 in the center, etc.
March 6th	7	4	1
April 5th	6	3	9
May 6th	5	2	8
June 6th	4	1	7
July 7th	3	9	6
Aug 8th	2	8	5
Sept 8th	1	7	4
Oct 8th	9	6	3
Nov 8th	8	5	2
Dec 8th	7	4	1
Jan 6th	6	3	9

the sequence of directions identical to the Construction Cycle Number and the Annual Number, from center to Northwest to West to Northeast to South to North to Southwest to East and then to Southeast. Then, month after month, the number in any particular direction will *descend* perpetually.

Notice also that the monthly energy does not start on the first day of our western calendar months. The monthly cycle begins anywhere from the 5th to the 8th of a given month.

Referring to the chart above, we can see that in the Year of the Ox and in the month of May, there is always a 2 Monthly Center Star. So, for a house that has a 2-1 in the center (permanent Mountain and Water Stars), that will always indicate a *monthly* People Lock for that house. In the Year of the Snake, we can see that the month of September has a Monthly 4 Star in the Center. So, if a house has 8-4 Center Stars (permanent Stars), it will be in a *one-month* Money Lock at those recurring times.

In order to fly all the Monthly Stars throughout each direction, just look at which star is in the center palace in any given month. Then, ascend the sequence of the numbers through each direction as you do the Period Star Numbers and the Annual Numbers.

For example, when you refer to the monthly chart, you can see that in the Year of the Rabbit, the month of May will have the 5 Star in the center palace. You can then proceed to place a monthly 6 Star in the Northwest, a monthly 7 Star in the West, a monthly 8 Star in Northeast, and then just follow the exact same ascension pattern through all the directions.

Chart for the Chinese Zodiac Sign of the Year

Rat: 1936, 1948, 1960, 1972, 1984, 1996, 2008, 2020, 2032, 2044, 2056, 2068

Ox: 1937, 1949, 1961, 1973, 1985, 1997, 2009, 2021, 2033, 2045, 2057, 2069

Tiger: 1938, 1950, 1962, 1974, 1986, 1998, 2010, 2022, 2034, 2046, 2058, 2070

Rabbit: 1939, 1951, 1963, 1975, 1987, 1999, 2011, 2023, 2035, 2047, 2059, 2071

Dragon: 1940, 1952, 1964, 1976, 1988, 2000, 2012, 2024, 2036, 2048, 2060, 2072

Snake: 1941, 1953, 1965, 1977, 1989, 2001, 2013, 2025, 2037, 2049, 2061, 2073

Horse: 1942, 1954, 1966, 1978, 1990, 2002, 2014, 2026, 2038, 2050, 2062, 2074

Sheep: 1943, 1955, 1967, 1979, 1991, 2003, 2015, 2027, 2039, 2051, 2063, 2075

Monkey: 1944, 1956, 1968, 1980, 1992, 2004, 2016, 2028, 2040, 2052, 2064, 2076

Rooster: 1945, 1957, 1969, 1981, 1993, 2005, 2017, 2029, 2041, 2053, 2065, 2077

Dog: 1946, 1958, 1970, 1982, 1994, 2006, 2018, 2030, 2042, 2054, 2066, 2078

Pig: 1947, 1959, 1971, 1983, 1995, 2007, 2019, 2031, 2043, 2055, 2067, 2079

It should be noted that in Feng Shui and in Four Pillars Chinese astrology (Zi Ping), the Chinese *solar* calendar is used, *not* the Chinese *lunar* calendar. The Chinese lunar calendar will vacillate from year to year depending on what day it begins on a western calendar. But with the Chinese solar calendar, the beginning day is always February 4th or February 5th, just varying from year to year by hours and minutes. To find out exactly what time on any given February 4th the new solar year begins, you can consult a book called the *Chinese 10,000 Year Solar Calendar*. This information can also be obtained from a Chinese astrologer, who will have this calendar in his or her possession.

This February 4th/5th starting date is the exact midway point between the winter solstice and the spring equinox. It should not be confused with the lunar calendar. There are, however, many Feng Shui books that print the Lunar Calendar. This means someone could be born between January 21st and February 20th in any given year and be classified under a certain zodiac sign according to the lunar calendar but not the solar calendar. Use the solar calendar beginning date of February 4th/5th unless you are studying a branch of Chinese astrology called Zi Wei Dou Shu. That school of astrology is based on lunar cycles. This might seem confusing, but look at our own western calendar. We still celebrate a number of holidays based on a lunar calendar, which is why the date of the holiday changes from year to year, such as Passover and Easter. They are being observed in accordance with a lunar calendar overlapping our solar calendar.

CURES FOR THE LOCKED PERIODS

There are several cures for the Locked Periods of a house, and they can help whether the Locked Period is long-term, short-term, a People Lock, or a Money Lock.

The most effortless cure might already be in place for a house that has an open floor plan. If you can walk from the front door in a straight line right to the center of your house, *with no walls to obstruct a direct path,* then this floor plan helps the house not be in such an iron-clad Locked Period.

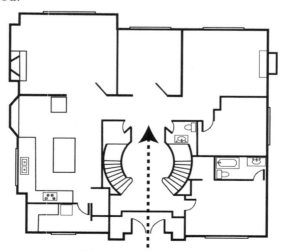

FIGURE 5A shows a house with an open floor plan so that a straight line can go from the front door to the center.

Also effortless and lucky in this regard is a house that has a close and constant view of water. Homes that are right on the beach often bypass the Locked Periods. But the water has to be very prominent in the experience of living in that house type. It is not enough just to live in a beach community with the ocean ten blocks away. Your home would literally have to be on the coastline with a close, perpetual view of the water to escape the effects of a Locked Period. As well, a house that is right on a lake can avoid the Locked Periods. It should not be construed that a house very close to water is immune from having any problems. In fact, a house can be considered too close to water for other reasons. It is just the Locked Periods that are dealt with automatically.

For the house that does not have a large body of water already very close by, occupants need to create water features inside and/or outside their home so they can hear and see the water regularly. There are a number of water formulae used for other reasons, which can also do double duty to release a Lock. For example, if you have a Reversed House that needs water behind it for the long term, then this same water feature could help release a Lock. Or, if you had placed a water fountain at a 4-7 entrance for the sake of curing that particular area of your home, it could also work to release the Lock for the entire house if the water source is big enough. The basic prescription is that you need to be able to hear and see circulating water. Photographs of water or blue color will not work. Real water is needed.

Another way to cure a Lock is to fortify the location of a Mountain Star 5 with Water when a house is in a twenty-year People Lock. And if the house is in a twenty-year Money Lock, you can add Water to the location of the Water Star 5. *This is a definite departure from Five-Element theory* because the 5 Star is Earth-type energy and, strictly speaking, will dominate Water. But the 5 Star is always a bit of a chameleon and longs always to "go home" to the center. So, wherever the Mountain Star 5 is in your home, it is identifying with the Mountain Star in the center palace. Wherever the Water Star 5 is in your home, it is also identifying with the Water Star in the center palace.

Referring to the chart below, you have a 4-8 combination in the center of this Period 6, West 1 facing house. The 1-5 combination is in the Northeast. That particular Water Star 5 is identifying with the energy of the 8 Water Star in the Center.

NE 1-5	E 6-1	SE 5-9
9	4	5
N 8-3	4-8	S 9-4
2	6	1
NW 3-7	W 2-6	SW 7-2
7	8	3

V

Only when the 5 Star is identifying with a *Wang Star in the center* can you add Water to the 5 Star to help release the Lock. Notice in the chart above the 5-9 combination in the Southeast. That Mountain Star 5 is identifying with the energy of the 4 Mountain Star in the center. But the 4 Star is not in a Wang phase in Period 8. So you do not add Water to the 5-9 Southeast area. You would still add Metal to cure the basic nature of the 5 Star. Since both of the 5 Stars in this chart are "masquerading" as better Stars, we could say the chart is slightly better in those areas. Conversely, there will be other charts where the 5 Mountain Star and 5 Water Star in some part of the house will be mimicking a 2, 3, or 7 Star from the center, which is not as good. It is like another subtle layer of meaning to the 5 Star.

The only time you should use Water with a 5 Star is when you are trying to unlock a twenty-year Lock. It is *not used* to unlock a one-year or monthly Lock. So do not use the Water remedy with the 5 Star if it is going to be in conflict with an annual or monthly cycle. There are even more formulae for releasing a Lock. One other formula consists of using Fire in an unconventional way. Some of these formulae should only be used by experienced Feng Shui practitioners. Just using Water can be very effective and will create less potential for side effects.

STRING OF PEARLS HOUSE
(LIN CHU PAN KUA)

This house type always gets highlighted in classical Feng Shui books, but there seems to be confusion about its effects. Some schools teach that this house is lucky. Others teach that it is an unlucky house, particularly for an elderly woman (which means over sixty.)

The String of Pearls house is a Flying Star chart where the number flow from Mountain Star to Period Star to Water Star is a sequential series of numbers in every single direction. So the series of numbers could be 1, 2, 3 or 4, 5, 6 or 7, 8, 9.

Look at the chart below to see this sequential series of numbers in each directional sector. This is a Period 5 house that faces Northwest 2. As an example, the East sector holds the 2-3-4 series, and the West holds the sequence 6-7-8.

In order for a house to qualify as the String of Pearls House, every single sector has to have the sequential arrangement. The theory continues that if the house numbers ascend toward the Water Star position, then it is a particularly good house for money luck. But if the sequence of numbers ascends toward the Mountain Star, then the house is supposed to be particularly good for people luck. Personally, I have not seen this house type be extraordinarily lucky. The String of Pearls houses I have seen do not live up to their reputation, and that might be because of another theory, which states this house type is lucky only within the Period in which it was built. The example below also happens to be a Period 5 house and a Reversed House on top of that. By the time I started evaluating these house types, it was already Period 7.

There are String of Pearl houses in other eras, not just the Period 5.

E 2-4 3	SE 3-5 4	S 8-1 9
NE 7-9 8	4-6 5	SW 1-3 2
N 9-2 1	NW 5-7 6	W 6-8 7

V

3 PERIOD HOUSE (AKA PARENT STRING) OR FU MU SAN GUA

This house also gets a mixed review. Some people think this house is so lucky that you do not have to perform any remedies on it, but that is seriously faulty thinking. Other schools regard this house as "high drama," in which there are more substantial variances from year to year showcasing the fortunes and misfortunes of the occupants.

The code for deciphering the 3 Period House is to look at each directional sector to see whether there is a representative from each of the 3 major sixty-year Cycles described earlier in this book. The Upper Yuan defines Periods 1, 2, and 3. The Middle Yuan holds Period 4, 5, and 6. And the Lower Yuan represents Periods 7, 8, and 9. If each directional area has one Star that comes from each of these Upper, Middle, and Lower Yuan Eras, then the house will perpetually be a "3 Period House." No matter what Period we are in, there will always be one Star out of the three that is considered Sheng or Wang. When looking at all the three Stars together, I like Master Sang's metaphor that it is like a room with three women. Two of the women are old and one is young, fresh, and attractive. In other words, there is something always lively and fortunate in each area. The chart below is for a Period 4 House that faces SW 1 and sits NE 1.

N 3-6 9	NE 1-4 7	E 5-8 2
NW 8-2 5	7-1 4	SE 6-9 3
W 9-3 6	SW 4-7 1	S 2-5 8

V

Notice that each sector has some combination of 2-5-8 or 3-6-9 or 1-4-7. In Period 8, the Wang and Sheng numbers are 8, 9, and 1. Since every sector has an 8, 9, or 1 Star, there is something Wang or Sheng about every area. In Period 9, the Wang and Sheng numbers will be 9,

1, and 2. Again, each sector will have a 9, 1, or 2 Star, and the house will be perpetually lucky. Using the exact same chart, you can also glean even more information about the potential effects on the occupants and whether this house is really lucky or whether it will be more of a "high-drama" house.

- By looking at the Center Stars we can see that in the last Period 7 (1984–2003) this house was in a twenty-year People Lock.

- Looking at the sitting and facing palaces and the position of the 4 Star in each of these palaces, we can also see that this house is Reversed Type.

- Going back to the Center Stars, you have learned in Chapter Three that 7-1 in the center can indicate an occupant can have a penchant for drinking or have other addictive behaviors. Now, just how lucky do you think this house type is? I think this house type can be lucky for some and not for others!

COMBINATION OF 10 HOUSE

This house type is also considered special and lucky. The way to identify this chart is by looking at the combination of the Period Star with either the Mountain Star or the Water Star in each and every directional area. Below is an example of a SW 1 sitting house/NE 1 facing and built in Period 8.

S 1-7 3	SW 8-5 5	W 3-9 1
SE 6-3 7	5-2 8	NW 4-1 9
E 7-4 6	NE 2-8 2	N 9-6 4

V

- In the center sector the Period Star 8 plus the Water Star 2 = 10.
- In the Southwest sector the Period Star 5 plus the Water Star 5 = 10.

- In the West sector the Period Star 1 plus the Water Star 9 = 10.
- In the Northwest sector the Period Star 9 plus the Water Star 1 = 10.
- In the North sector the Period Star 4 plus the Water Star 6 = 10.
- In the Northeast sector the Period Star 2 plus the Water Star 8 = 10.
- In the East sector the Period Star 6 plus the Water Star 4 = 10.
- In the Southeast sector the Period Star 7 plus the Water Star 3 = 10.
- In the South sector the Period Star 3 plus the Water Star 7 = 10.

This "Combination of 10" House must have the 10 combination in every single sector. If the Period Star and the Water Star in each area add to 10, the house is especially lucky for money. If the Period Star and the Mountain Star in each area add to 10, the house is especially good for People Luck. Don't confuse "luck" for "lock."

Below is an example of a "Combination of 10" House where the Mountain Stars and Period Stars make it extra fortunate for people luck. This is a house that sits West1/faces East1 and was built in Period 4.

SW 9-5 1	W 4-9 6	NW 5-1 5
S 2-7 8	6-2 4	N 1-6 9
SE 7-3 3	E 8-4 2	NE 3-8 7

V

There are "Combination of 10" Houses in every Period. In Chapter Four's section on Wang Shan Wang Shui house types, look up the Period 2 SW 1 sitting or the NE 1 sitting house, and you will see another example of a "Combination of 10" House.

HIDDEN AND INVERSE SIREN

There are a few house types that have a 5 Star in the center Mountain Star position or the center Water Star position. If the 5 Star is in the center Mountain Star position, the house can be considered especially bad for people. If the 5 Star is in the center Water Star position, the house can be considered especially bad for career luck. This is because the 5 Star is in the "soul" of the house, the center palace. If the Stars ascend in their numerical pattern, this chart is called the Hidden Siren. If the Stars descend in their numerical pattern, this chart is called the Inverse Siren.

Even though this house type is considered problematic, it can be neutralized with all the Feng Shui corrections. In fact, the example below shows an Inverse Siren House type that is actually Wang Shan Wang Shui. This chart is for Period 7, East 1 sitting.

NE 2-6	E 7-2	SE 6-1
1	5	6
N 9-4	5-9	S 1-5
3	7	2
NW 4-8	W 3-7	SW 8-3
8	9	4

v

OUT-OF-TRIGRAM HOUSE

This house type is both defined and remedied differently according to various schools of Feng Shui. "Out-of-Trigram" refers to a house type that has an indefinite compass reading. This is when a building sits and faces a direction that rests right on the line between two different directions. There are eight basic directions, so there are eight major directions right in between them. For example, if a house faces or sits 67.5 degrees, that is the exact cut-off point between Northeast and East. Below is a chart that shows the Out-of-Trigram cut-off points.

Exact Degree Cut-Off Point	Between the Major Directions
67.5	NE / E
112.5	E / SE
157.5	SE / S
202.5	S / SW
247.5	SW/ W
292.5	W /NW
337.5	NW / N
22.5	N/ NE

The chart above shows the major "evil lines" as they are sometimes referred to in older books. But there are also minor Out-of-Trigram lines, which always exist between the first and second sector of any direction. It is frustrating for all who do a compass reading to find the correct orientation between the first and second sectors. By studying the four major house types, this confusion about which orientation is accurate can mean the difference between a Wang Shan Wang Shui House and a Reversed House. It can also mean the difference between a Double Sitting House and a Double Facing House.

But the Major Lines are what is most frequently discussed. Some schools will allow for as much as a couple of degrees on either side of the cut-off point to identify the house type as Out-of-Trigram. This never made much sense to me because if you can actually distinguish the orientation by a couple of degrees, then it seems like it would not be truly Out-of-Trigram. For example, if 202.5 degrees is the cut-off point between South and Southwest and your reading clearly says 200 degrees without wavering at various distances from the property, then it seems like you should be comfortable calling that 200 degrees just inside of South. Or you could do a comparative reading for South 3 and Southwest 1 and get feedback about which chart rings most true.

Some people doubt that an Out-of-Trigram House even exists, insisting that a house *must* be aligned with one of the two sectors it sits between, even if it is not readily obvious which one it is. This might be true, but the closeness to the cut-off point has revealed to me that something is not quite right with this special house type. I have seen over and over again that people who live in these Out-of-Trigram Houses will suffer from mental problems or at least one of their house mates will suffer from mental problems. I've seen clients in this house type with everything from schizophrenia, bipolar disorder, depression, unfounded relentless worrying, obsessive-compulsive disorder, or misfortunes that cannot be explained in any other way. Their houses often do not respond to remedies for *either* of the two possible house types that the house sits in between.

Some schools teach that if a house appears to be Out-of-Trigram, then a completely different set of Flying Star charts called *Substitution Stars* or *Replacement Stars* should be used. I have seen these Replacement Star charts, and they don't make much sense to me. I know of some very good Feng Shui teachers who include the Replacement Star formulae in their curricula, but I have elected not to use them. Initially I applied them to a few house types that appeared Out-of-Trigram, but the clients did not give me feedback that these readings rang true to their experience in their own dwellings. I tend to think that a house type truly Out-of-Trigram might not have any defined Flying Star chart, much the way outside space does not have a Flying Star chart except in the most subtle kind of influence like what I describe in the next chapter regarding open spaces. I have several suggestions for how to approach a house type that appears to be Out-of-Trigram.

1. Take numerous compass readings from all four sides of the structure to get a consensus whether there is any particular reading more consistent than others.

2. Use more than one compass to get your readings and stand at various distances from the sitting and facing walls. As a practitioner, I always carry two compasses with me in the event that I will need to compare their readings.

3. Do a Flying Star chart based on the sitting direction of the structure if that side of the house gets a more consistent reading than the facing side.

4. If the house seems hopelessly fixed sitting and facing right on one of the major cut-off points, then do a comparative reading of the two possibilities on behalf of the occupant and ask him or her for candid feedback to see whether one of the charts appears to be more accurate than another. Even an experienced practitioner with a good compass is hard pressed to pinpoint the reading down to one degree of accuracy.

5. If the person whose house appears Out-of-Trigram has just moved in and he or she has no significant history with the house, then try to find out what you can about the previous occupant's experiences in the house to see whether something stands out to align itself with one of the two charts you are comparing. For example, did the previous occupant become wealthy and move on to a bigger home? Or did the previous occupant have something really negative happen to him or her that matches the reading of one of the possible house types?

6. If it still becomes impossible to tell which chart is accurate, compare the two and see what they have in common. There will be at least a few things they will have in common and that are only good for both house types. For example, you might discover that one chart is a Reversed House Type and the other is Double Sitting; you could then feel confident about recommending Water in the back of either of those house types.

Finally, there is one very important tool you can use to help define which reading is accurate, and this can help you some of the time if you are dealing with a structure that is at least thirty years old: The magnetic declination of an area will change slowly over time. You could go to the National Geophysical Data Center website and look up what the magnetic declination of an area is currently as well as when it was first built (with statistics available going back to the year 1900). I have noticed that the magnetic declination might change in certain areas by 1 degree every twenty to forty years. If you are trying to evaluate a house that is even older, the magnetic declination may have changed by a few degrees, making it much easier to figure out what the compass reading was *at the time the structure was built.*

I once had a client living in a house built in 1895 in New York, and the magnetic compass reading had changed by 6 degrees westerly when the reading was evaluated in 2007. Those 6 degrees made a difference between a North 1 facing house and a North 2 facing house. Here is another example: Let us say you are looking at a house that currently sits 67.5 degrees in the year you do the reading. That is right on the line between Northeast and East. Let us say, arbitrarily, that you are doing a reading in an area where Magnetic North is 13 degrees East of True North; but when the house was built sixty years ago, the magnetic declination was 15 degrees East of True North. You could subtract 2 more degrees from your current reading and feel confident that the house was sitting 65.5 degrees when it was built, thus making it a Northeast-sitting house instead of right on the line (Out-of-Trigram) or East-sitting. You can try this method if you are very experienced doing compass readings with a high-quality compass. The inevitable question that comes up is: Why shouldn't we re-calculate the house according to what it presently is as opposed to what the compass reading was when it was built? In the next chapter I have a section about houses that have moved slightly on their foundations due to earthquakes or ground settling, and the same principle would apply. Of course, one could argue that while an area may have changed its magnetic declination slightly over time, a good strong earthquake could jolt the house in the opposite direction at any time. You should just do the best you can to figure out the original house type.

Downtown Los Angeles is just one area that challenges even the most experienced Feng Shui practitioner. Street by street, block by block, you have buildings that appear to sit very close to facing being between North 3 and NE 1 or between NE 1 and NE 2 as well as other borderline directions. But many of these buildings in question were built in the 1920s or earlier, and the compass reading for that particular zip code has changed a couple of degrees in the last eighty years. In addition, you are completely surrounded by huge metal buildings, and this alone can make the compass reading go haywire. You can assume that any large city or cluster of huge buildings will present this additional challenge to getting an accurate compass reading. Feng Shui practitioners are not psychics. We can only be as accurate as the information that is available to us. Do the best you can. And even though the emphasis of this book is on the Flying Stars, there are still other aspects to Feng Shui that are not dependent upon hair-splitting compass readings.

CENTER STARS

The Center Stars (aka Heaven's Heart) reflect the hidden agenda of each house type, which is why *The Feng Shui Matrix* includes a whole chapter devoted to what the center of each house means. The descriptions are nearly identical to what the Star combinations mean when they exist in any other sector, as described in Chapter Three.

For example, if you have 7-3 Center Stars in your house, it means the entire house is perpetually a little vulnerable to break-in, and home security should not be taken lightly. But if you have a 7-3 combination in any other part of the house, these Stars will not affect you as much unless they land in an area that is heavily used, such as an entrance or a bedroom. The difference with the Center Stars from other Stars is that they cannot really be remedied. They represent a constant potential for events or circumstances that an occupant might have to endure by living in that house type. For example, if the Center Stars are 7-3, an occupant will always have to be very careful about security in the home. But if the 7-3 combination is in another part of the house besides the center, that energy combination can be remedied with the fire element. It is disappointing to some Feng Shui enthusiasts and practitioners that not every single area of a house can be remedied with Five-Element theory or some other technique.

In fact, even when the center palace of a house is physically not included in the architecture, there is still an overlay of those Flying Stars spread throughout the house.

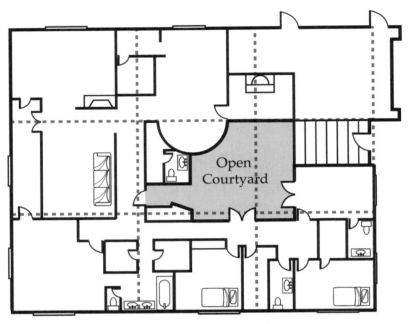

FIGURE 5B shows a house with a missing center palace.

CHAPTER SIX

Different Theories and Influences on the Stars

There are many schools of Feng Shui and many theories behind them, some old and some new. Even under the one umbrella of classical Feng Shui there are differences of opinion, so the point of this chapter is simply to expose you to these various theories. Historically, some false schools were created in order to keep the power of Feng Shui from being disseminated among the masses. Because of that, some false schools and theories have been perpetuated knowingly or unknowingly. In this chapter I will highlight some of the more common theories and ideas, even those that appear to contradict each other.

DATE OF OCCUPANCY

This theory is based on the notion that the house will change its essential Flying Stars based on when an occupant or family moves into a house. The same would be true for new tenants in a commercial building. It suggests that people have the power to transform the Feng Shui of a space just by their own uniqueness and personal energy. It is an interesting theory, but I don't personally give it much credence. An example of this would be taking a house that was built in Period 5 but calculating it as a Period 7 house if that was when the most recent occupants moved in. I have met with thousands of clients who have moved into their residences or places of work decades after its construction, and they still experience what is revealed by the Flying Star chart from the Construction Period of that space. In fact, when I corroborate the yearly and monthly cycles of a particular area of a house in conjunction with the Construction Year Chart, it is often stunningly specific, so I have a lot of confidence in using the Construction Cycle Stars as the basic template for the house.

When I was first introduced to the date of occupancy theory, I reviewed many client files and saw that if I had advised the clients with remedies based on when they moved in, instead of when the house was built, then I would have advised them very differently, and they would not have gotten the predictably good results they got by my having gone with the original construction date of the property. In the mid-1990s there was a very popular Feng Shui teacher who taught that if a person emptied out his or her house and moved out for three months and then moved back in, this process could change the Construction Period of the house. I have never asked a client to do this to validate the results. If any Feng Shui practitioner reading this uses the date of occupancy theory and has lots of case study evidence to back it up as valid, I would love to hear about it, genuinely. Another notion is that if you remove a certain number of tiles from the roof that you can achieve the same effect. That ritual seems even more far-fetched.

CURRENT ERA CHART

Another theory about timing involves looking at each structure with the Flying Star chart from the current era that we are living in. This would mean that no matter when the structure was built, the Flying Star chart used would be from the current twenty-year era at the time of the reading. This theory contradicts the date of occupancy theory, which hands a lot of power over to the occupant and his or her ability to change a house's Feng Shui. The current period chart for everyone suggests that we all succumb to a greater power and that there is less variation in anyone's Feng Shui if all structures change every twenty years. Based on the 9 Periods and the 16 different possible orientations, there are 144 different Flying Star charts. The current era theory would indicate that all structures can only perpetually be one of 16 different chart types. Some people use this theory exclusively, which I think is just as much of a mistake as using the date of occupancy theory exclusively. I do think, instead, that we could consider an overlay of the current era chart along with the original construction year chart. According to Master Sang, you can glance at the current era chart to see what hidden meaning might be underneath the basic disposition of the house. This might be the equivalent of a natal astrology chart with an overlay of a progressive chart.

Master Sang stated once in an Institute Society Meeting that one should remedy a house with appropriate remedies for the Construction Period of the house but also glean more insight by glancing at the current era chart. On that day, we were at the home of a couple who had the 4-6 Flying Stars in their bedroom, and the remedy was for water in the room to cure the domination cycle of 6 Metal destroying 4 Wood. This was based on it being a Period 7 construction. By also noting the Period 8 overlay, the master bedroom had a 2 Star in the room, so Master Sang suggested they *not* try to conceive in this room. (A permanent 2 Star in a bedroom can contribute to miscarriage or birth defects.) And the 4-6 combination from the original construction chart could predict a difficult pregnancy since the 4 Star is related to the hip and pelvis area.

Another example of comparing the construction cycle chart with the current era chart: Let us say there is a bedroom with the 1-4 Star combination, based on when the house was built. This can indicate a potential for infidelity. Now, if the current era chart for that area had an overlay of the 6-3 Flying Stars, then the complications of the "infidelity" energy could take on legal ramifications or generate gossip because of the additional 3 Star from the current era chart overlay.

CHANGING THE PERIOD CHART

Changing the Period of a house through remodeling is something that can puzzle even a very experienced practitioner. There are a few guidelines to follow, but it is as if each remodel might need to be viewed on a case-by-case basis. In fact, this is one of the few times that a consultant might need to rely on intuition, unless the after-effects of the remodel have already been documented. Some remodels are easier to figure out than others. When a house is basically gutted and brought down to the framing or left with just one wall standing, that most definitely necessitates a new chart for the house. Of course, if a drastic remodel occurs within the same twenty-year era in which it was originally built, then the only thing that might change are the dimensions of the *same* Flying Star chart if the dimensions of the house have changed. Changing the era of a house through remodeling is based mostly on whether the qi in the house can easily escape from large gaping holes where new rays of sun can beam into the structure.

When a very large portion of the ceiling is opened up to the sky, it can create a new chart for the house. The size of the opening needed to change the Flying Star chart is subject to debate. Certainly, if a third or more of the ceiling is open to the sky, that could allow new energies to enter the house. Some also believe that if a huge skylight is placed in the center of the house that it should change the qi. An ordinary skylight would not change the qi of a house, but one that had very large dimensions in the center, such as ten square feet or more, could work. I also think that if a house or building has numerous skylights put in at the same time it could yield a new chart as well. I have looked at quite a few buildings in Santa Monica that were originally built in Period 4 but have been substantially remodeled in Period 7 with numerous large skylights, and they have taken on the newer cycle's personality.

Expanding the size of a room by pushing it out as much as twenty feet or so will not change the construction chart for the whole house. Instead, it is more like the same qi seeping into the expanded space like a person gaining weight. This is especially true if there is a wide opening to the expanded space. But if you have a room added to a house with just an ordinary three-foot-wide doorway, then you might consider the room addition to be its own mini-house attached to the original.

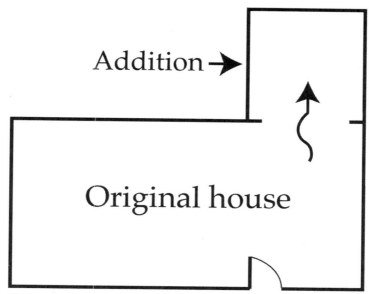

FIGURE 6A. The illustration in Fig. 6A shows an addition with a wide opening.

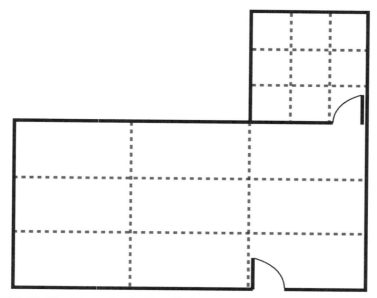

FIGURE 6B. The illustration in Fig. 6B shows an addition with a narrow opening.

Technically, by removing a large enough section of the roof and ceiling, you can let enough rays of the sun into the space through to the bottom floor to create a new cycle. But what happens if a house has severe fire damage inside without the roof coming off?

I have worked with people in this circumstance, and if the fire has been contained to a small area of the house, then the original cycle remains. But if the smoke and fire damage was extensive, then we could say that the qi was "choked off" and ruined. A new cycle of the house will be created when all the surfaces change due to smoke damage. Otherwise, just doing internal remodeling, even moving walls around, will not change the cycle of the house. The key is the pervasiveness of the smoke.

I once had a client whose home was opened up quite a bit during a remodel. A very large exterior wall, about twenty feet high, was removed. The house was left open for months. Then, the neighborhood experienced a large brush fire. Even though my client's house was not in the actual fire, the smoke was suffocating, and the neighborhood had to be evacuated. As it was a horse ranch area, both people and animals had to be evacuated. So, smoke blew through the house and left a lot of ash behind. To top it off, even though the house did not have its ceiling opened to the sky, it was so opened up to the elements because of the lack of walls that birds nested in the house while it was under renovation for more than a year. This is the kind of house that has been totally transformed by an event. Also, while writing this book, I advised a client whose home had been flooded by Hurricane Katrina. Water levels rose to over five feet inside the house, so there had to be extensive remodeling. To add insult to injury, the side of the house was hit by a tornado the same year. This house was originally built in Period 7, but after Hurricane Katrina did its extensive damage (2005), it had to be recalculated as a Period 8 House.

MOVING A HOUSE

Certainly, when a house is picked up off its foundation and moved to another location, it is like unplugging an appliance and then plugging it back in at the new location. Often, a house that is moved will also be cut in half and put back together on the new lot. But even if the whole house were removed intact, it would take on a new Flying Star chart for the new direction it would face and the new timing of its placement. Actually moving the entire house could be seen as the most radical of all remodels.

FIRST FLOOR VERSUS SECOND FLOOR

When I first began my Feng Shui practice, I really felt it was possible for a house to have a Flying Star chart on the top floor that was distinct from the bottom floor if the second floor was added without opening up the first floor by more than just a normal sized staircase. Feng Shui practitioners can argue this point, and sometimes it can really be nerve racking trying to figure out how the qi moves. It is easy to talk about qi-flow in an academic or theoretic way, but some places have to be dealt with on a case-by-case basis. Since the Flying Stars are a combination of earthly and heavenly influences, it is difficult to know for sure what has more weight when a second story is added on without opening up much of the ceiling to the first floor. And yet, there is an opening. The energies from the sun and stars will penetrate downward onto the second-story construction, but they will not be able to reach the ground under the first floor. Does that matter?

Also, what if the first floor ceiling is opened up *after* the ceiling of the second floor is sealed up? And what happens when someone encloses an area underneath a house that is perched over a cliff. Eventually, a Feng Shui practitioner will visit a home where a dug-out area under the house will have been enclosed to form a new room *under* an existing part of the house. Here you have the direct influence of the earth but not the sky. In the same way that the Flying Star chart repeats itself on every floor in a multi-story building, we can assume that if a second story is added that the original qi from the ground floor of the house will seep upward until the last or highest roof is installed. And if a room is added below, that energy can move downward as well. We might even speculate that the Stars get weaker with the more stories they have to envelope.

The exception to this guideline is if the remodel makes the house *more than twice its original size.* This, by definition, would include square footage that is part of a new foundation and, therefore, would put the whole house into a new mixture of time and space energies.

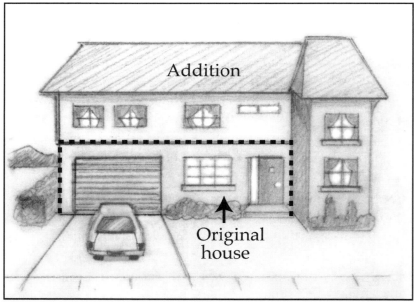

FIGURE 6C. The illustration in Fig. 6C is of a house with a second-story addition that completely covers the original first floor and that also adds more new one- and two-story space on the side of the original house.

CHANGING THE COMPASS ORIENTATION OF A HOUSE

Changing the orientation of a structure would have to involve a radical remodel. Many years ago, the American Feng Shui Institute had a society meeting at a restaurant that had formerly been a flower shop. It was the same building, but instead of an entrance on the street side, the restaurant now had its main entrance on the parking lot side, opposite the street. In addition, the interiors were completely redone, with a kitchen as well as seating, whereas the flower shop had just been one big room with a concrete floor. This radical change in the *function* of the space and the new double-entry doors convinced Master Sang to change the *orientation part* of the calculation but to keep it as the original Period 5 Construction Cycle since the ceiling had not been opened up to the sky and no exterior walls had been touched. These kinds of circumstances always fascinate me because the implication is that the qi has intelligence and understands when it is being radically altered.

In order for this to be valid, the remodel must be radical with many interior changes as well. Conversely, if a residential house eventually became a doctor's office (with former bedrooms used as treatment rooms), then that would not be a radical enough change to justify new calculations of time or direction. My son's first pediatrician had converted an old Craftsman-style home into his office, and I've since seen many times where a residence ends up being used for commercial purposes without changing the Period chart of the structure or its orientation.

SOUTHERN HEMISPHERE THEORY

Feng Shui has been practiced for thousands of years, but only in the 1990s did a new theory emerge about the Southern Hemisphere. Most of the continents are in the Northern Hemisphere, but it was an Australian man who launched a whole "Southern Hemisphere" movement. I have not yet heard of anyone who agrees with him, except for the graduate students he has trained at his own school. Even though the seasons are opposite of those in the Northern Hemisphere, that should not invalidate the flow of the Flying Stars. I have only done a few Feng Shui readings for people in the Southern Hemisphere, but reading the houses the same as if they were in the Northern Hemisphere has been successful.

One very experienced practitioner is Master Gayle Atherton, who resides in Sydney, Australia, and who probably has more experience than any other modern Feng Shui practitioner in doing readings in the

Southern Hemisphere. She has confirmed that you do not need to change the flow of the Flying Stars to accommodate the Southern Hemisphere. There is still an absolute North and South, and the opposing seasons of the year represent only a small aspect of the totality of yin-yang theory. Other Feng Shui scholars, both Asian and Western, have written articles available on the Internet about the faulty thinking behind the Southern Hemisphere theory.

SECTORS VERSUS LUO SHU SQUARES

When people peruse Feng Shui books with floor plans, they often become confused with the various ways that the directional sectors get divided up on the floor plan. The main camps include the "pie-shaped method" and the luo shu square method. There are a few others, but those are the main two. Unless the shape of a building is a perfect square, these directional sectors will end up in different parts of the floor plan, depending on which method you use.

The pie-shaped method seems more precise, and in *The Feng Shui Matrix* I gave many examples of special applications for using this method. These are often instances where a 15-degree increment is the total space to work with for correctly placing a remedy. According to Master Sang, the original application of the pie-shaped method was designated for gravesites. That is a whole branch of Feng Shui called Yin House Reading.

Deciding whether the pie-shaped method or the luo shu grid method should be used for floor plans should be based on the exterior walls of the structure. The vast majority of structures are some variation of a square or rectangle, so the luo shu grid method reflects that. The qi responds to the shape of the structure much like water will take on the shape of its container. If the exterior wall of a structure is, however, at least half curved or circular, then the qi configuration inside takes its cue from that, and you can use the pie-shaped method instead.

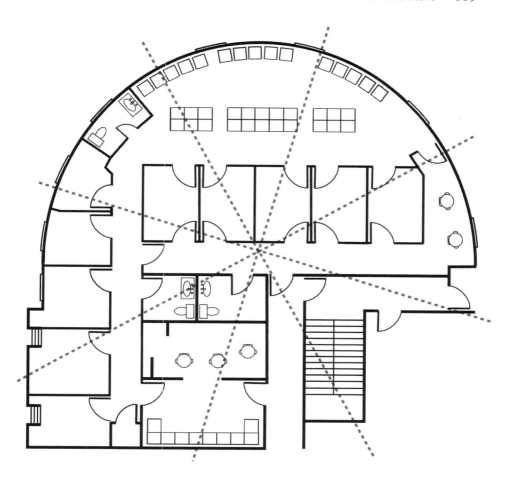

FIGURE 6D. The office shown in Fig. 6D has half its exterior wall as a half circle. This would justify dividing up the directional sectors into pie-shapes instead of luo shu squares.

CONSTRICTING OR CONFINING THE STARS

There are a few authors who teach that the Flying Stars can be contained by the walls in a room and that the division of the Flying Stars and directional sectors are *not* reliant on dividing up the floor plan in equal divisions, in terms of length and width.

FIGURE 6E is of a floor plan where smaller rooms contain the total influence of a Flying Star combination.

This theory supports the notion that walls are solid enough to contain and constrain the Stars. One well-known Feng Shui teacher says that you could even shove the bad Stars into a small confined area after the fact (and not affect the whole room) if you just build out a closet to the room. I do not personally adhere to this theory. And yet, we do call them *Flying* Stars, so I suppose anything is possible. I believe instead that the Flying Stars span through walls, so I divide up the directional sectors of the house according to the dimensions of the *exterior* walls. I believe that two rooms can share the same Flying Stars if the two rooms straddle one directional sector. So I have never suggested to a client that he or she could add a closet to a room to hold the bad Stars hostage there. The illustration below shows how a person might sleep and work in the same Flying Stars if the dimensions of his or her space allow for the sector in question to straddle two rooms.

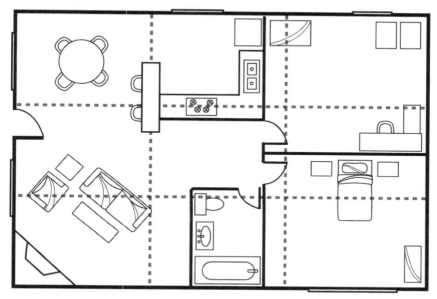

FIGURE 6F. In Fig. 6F a person could sleep with his or her headboard against a wall with a desk on the other side of the wall, all in the same sector.

MOBILE HOMES AND HOUSES NOT BUILT COMPLETELY ON THE GROUND

Mobile homes, houses built high over land on support pillars, and raised foundations are technically not built on the ground. Some Feng Shui schools place much emphasis on such technicalities as the rays of the sun having to hit the ground under a house while it's being built and the first floor of the house needing to be literally on the ground to create the Flying Stars inside. I have seen, however, that homes not firmly built on the ground still read like houses built on the ground. I use the same criteria of what direction the house sits and when the house was either built or positioned on the land. Some schools recommend using just the East/West school or something called the House Trigram Number for mobile homes or houses that have been moved. My liberal attitude about this is supported by other teachings imparted by Master Sang that allow us even to assess a piece of land without any structure on it using the Flying Star method.

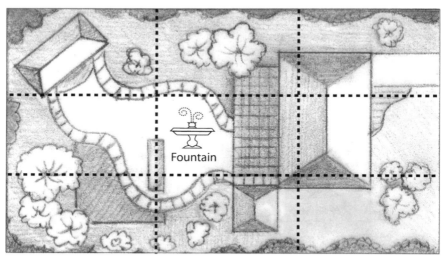

FIGURE 6G shows a small house and lot over which the luo shu grid has been superimposed.

One very memorable society meeting took place at the home of a landscape designer who had a tiny house on a much bigger lot. Students placed the luo shu grid over the floor plan, and we all agreed she needed Water in the center of her house. But Master Sang stepped in to say that the center of her house was really the center of the lot and not just the literal center of the house. This landscape designer had created a lush garden in her backyard, benches to sit on, little paths to roam, and meditation spots, and it was anchored by a little studio office at the back of the property. Master Sang concluded that she had made her outside living space as much a part of her home as the inside space, so the center was adjusted to reflect that. Remedying a house with elements using a grid over the whole lot rarely happens, but there are in fact exceptions to the rules, and this chapter could easily have been titled "Anything Can Happen."

FLYING STAR CHART FOR OPEN LAND

If you should be involved in the design phase of a new structure, be it residential or commercial, and there is quite a bit of land to work with, you can superimpose a Flying Star chart over the entire parcel in order to find out where the best areas will be for building. The catch is that you have to be very sure the structure or group of structures will be built within the Period for which you are doing the chart. You will also need to determine absolutely what the sitting and facing of the parcel will be, which is not always easy to do if there are no definitive land-scape features, surrounding structures, or roads already paved to identify the likely sitting and facing directions.

But let's create a hypothetical scenario in order to illustrate this point. Let's say you've been asked to assist in the design phase of a new high school that will be built in Period 9. You also know for sure what direction the high school (as a whole compound) will face and can arbitrarily decide that it will face toward the street. Individual buildings on the campus might face a variety of orientations, but at this point you can just look at *the entire campus as a whole*. Now, let us say that the campus will face South 2 and for sure be built in Period 9. Below is the chart for a North 2 sitting/South 2 facing chart for Period 9.

NW 4-5	N 9-9	NE 2-7
1	5	3
W 3-6	5-4	E 7-2
2	9	7
SW 8-1	S 1-8	SE 6-3
6	4	8

V

This chart can be superimposed over the land where the school will be built. It will *not* be more important than the individual Flying Star charts for actual buildings, but it can be used as a reference for where to place the buildings and where to have open space for a football field or a parking lot. Ideally, you would leave the "negative" areas or the less auspicious areas as outside space. This "parcel" chart will be a Double Sitting chart, which is pretty good for a school. It is inherently good for people, and that is more important for a school than the status of being "good for money." In Period 9, the 9, 1, and 2 Stars will be the most positive. But the 8 Star, which is an inherently good Star, will not all of a sudden turn bad in Period 9. So we can consider the location of the 8 Star an additional good area for classrooms, the administration building, the library, and any other buildings on the land. The very center area will be the 5-4 zone, so perhaps that can be an open courtyard area. The Southwest, South, and North areas will be the best for buildings because they will resonate with the 8, 9, and 1 Stars on a very subtle level. Next are the Northeast and East sectors because the 2 Star will become positive (sheng) starting in 2024. The South sector of the land might be a good area for the entrance into the campus since the Period 4 Star is in that area and the 4 Star is perpetually associated with academia and the arts. This is just an example of doing an overlay chart on land when you know what will eventually be the orientation of the whole parcel.

A HOUSE THAT SHIFTS ON ITS FOUNDATION

If a house shifts on its foundation due to an earthquake, it depends on how much the house moves in order to determine whether you re-calculate it or not. If a house shifts a few degrees, then you can continue to consider it the original reading. One time a woman from another country emailed me to say that after an earthquake in her city, her house shifted from being a Southwest 1 facing house to Southwest 2 facing. She said it moved about 5 degrees. It seemed to me that the house should continue to maintain its original qi. I checked with Master Sang for his opinion, and he had a perfect metaphor to confirm what I was thinking. He said that if you have an appliance plugged into an electrical socket and it shifts a little, the appliance is still plugged into the socket and still has the current going through it. Many of you have seen an unbalanced load of laundry make a washing machine shake violently and even turn a bit. And yet it remains spinning and working. It is the same concept with a foundation that moves a bit.

Now, for sure, if a house shifts on its foundation by 30 or more degrees, there is a good chance that it has also sustained enough damage in other areas that it might need to be considered to have a new construction cycle or a new orientation considering how substantial the repairs would be. Houses generally do not move that much unless other significant damage also occurs, thus qualifying for the "radical" remodel.

TURNING A MOUNTAIN STAR INTO A WATER STAR

There are many mysterious theories that are also difficult to explain in mundane terms. Some of the most secret advanced cures are really wild, such as the one about to be described. Is it possible to turn a Mountain Star into a Water Star? One set of applications says "yes" if you take special care in the furniture arrangement of a room. Let us say that your home office is in an 8-3 sector, *with the room in any house being a miniature version of the whole house.* That said, if the sitting side of a house is the East side, then you could consider the East wall of every room in that house to be the sitting side of the room. Now, when you look toward the sitting wall of the office, the left side of the room will be the mountain side and the right side of the room will be the facing side. If you had a home office that was 8-3 and you wanted to turn it into a 3-8 arrangement, you could put higher, taller objects on the facing side (right-hand side) of the room. Remember, your reference of what is the left or right side of the room is in relation to the sitting side of the room. Since taller objects (like bookshelves) and file cabinets are "virtual mountains," by definition the other side of the room becomes lower, which is "virtual Water." Then, that 8-3 room will have virtual Water on the 8 side and a virtual mountain on the 3 side. By having Water (lower level) on the 8 side, you can make the 8 Mountain Star function like a Water Star. For an office it is more important to have the prosperity star in the Water Star position instead of the Mountain Star position.

FIGURE 6H shows a home office where bookshelves on one side act as mountains.

When Master Sang taught this method many years ago, he also said that a person could put his or her desk up on a platform on the side of the room that needed to be more mountainous. By creating more mountain energy in this area, the lower part of the room becomes the virtual Water. This could be a way to flip a 9-6 room into a 6-9 arrangement or to flip a 1-7 room into a 7-1 area.

Now, for a room like the bedroom where the Mountain Star is more influential, you would want to do the opposite. Let us say you had a bedroom with 2-8 Flying Stars and you would prefer the 8 Star be in the Mountain Star position. Let's arbitrarily say that the house sits Northeast. Therefore, the Northeast wall in each room in the house would be the sitting side. Stand in this room facing the sitting side wall. To your left is the Mountain Star side of the room and to your right is the Water Star side of the room.

Put something on the right side of the room that is tall, something with height to create a virtual mountain, and make that 8 Water Star in the room feel more like a mountain. If the bed is on that side of the room for other good reasons, you could put the bed on a platform (even just a couple of inches high) and that can turn the 8 Water Star into an 8 Mountain Star.

FIGURE 6I. The illustration in Fig. 6I is of a bedroom where the bed is on a platform.

This is admittedly a strange, subtle technique, and I have not been documenting or using this special technique on a regular basis. Sometimes there are just limitations to a room's layout, but if you are a serious Feng Shui practitioner, look for the opportunity to see whether you can turn a Mountain Star into a Water Star (or vice versa) and document it. Perhaps this can become as reliable a technique as the well-documented Water remedy for a Locked Period. Now, it is possible that changing the heights of objects in a room really won't turn a Water Star into a Mountain Star completely, but perhaps it can create a semblance of one in the same way that the 5 Star always behaves like a chameleon for the Center Stars without completely losing its identity as the 5 Star. This was discussed in Chapter Five regarding one of the cures for a twenty-year Locked Period.

PRIORITIES OF THE STARS

In this book you have learned about the advanced Flying Stars. That alone is enough to help you resolve many problems in your life. There are also annual influences that behave in similar ways, which I emphasized in *Feng Shui for Skeptics* and *The Feng Shui Matrix*. The Star patterns will overlap each other, and it does take a lot of practice to understand the manifestations of the combined influences. For instance, if a room has a 5-9 combination and an Annual 5 enters that area, it will obviously make things worse. But if the 5-9 area has an Annual 8 Star join the group, then that will make things a little better, as long as the permanent 5 Star is remedied with Metal. There are also Monthly Stars and Daily Stars, but they are not of much use to you unless you have a working knowledge of the advanced permanent Flying Stars. Here is an example of a Monthly Star's influence when combined with the permanent Stars.

- If you have a 7-3 advanced Flying Star combination (Mountain Star and Water Star) at your front door, it is an area that is vulnerable to a break-in.

- If an Annual 3 or 7 Star joins the permanent 7-3 combination, the likelihood of the break-in happening increases *for that year*.

- Then, if there were a Monthly 7 or 3 Star joining the group, it can often predict the exact month the break-in would occur. In fact, even a Monthly 1 Star could trigger the break-in because 1 Water will strengthen the 3 Wood Star. I have corroborated the effects of the Monthly, Yearly, and Permanent Stars combined in many scenarios.

The perpetual question that any Feng Shui student has is how to prioritize the influences. If you have an 8-6 bedroom, which is regarded as good, and then an Annual 5 star joins the 8-6 combination, must you add Metal to cure the Annual 5? Students ask this, knowing that the Metal cure will reduce the negatives of the 5 Earth Star but at the same time reduce the good qualities of the 8 Earth Star it is joined with. Which is more important? That answer can depend on even more variables, such as where do these Stars reside, who is using the room, and what is the function of the room.

The "location" means which sector. A 5 Star will not be quite so powerful in the Northwest or the West sectors because those directions are inherently Metal directions.

You could get away with adding fewer Metal cures to a 5 Star in the Northwest or West than if it resides in the South (inherently a Fire direction). Below is a chart that depicts the *inherent* element associated with each direction.

NW Metal	N Water	NE Earth
W Metal	Center Earth	E Wood
SW Earth	S South	SE Wood

This simple chart is full of meaning because each direction resonates with an element, a season, and a family member. You can review the symbolism of each direction and Trigram in Chapter Three. For example, the direction of Southeast is associated not only with Wood, but also with the eldest daughter in the family. Remember, this is the Post-Heaven Sequence. If a house were missing its Southeast sector, then there could be something deficient or problematic with the eldest daughter living in that house. But it is this same chart that gets misinterpreted by the less comprehensive schools of Feng Shui. A person who does not know more than these Element/Direction assignments might make the error of always placing red-colored objects in the South and a water fountain in the North. This is overly simplistic and possibly harmful based on what you have already learned in this book because there are so many other influences, including the advanced Flying Stars.

Referring to the simple Direction/Element Chart, you can see that the Southeast is inherently related to the Wood element. If a Flying Star pattern 4-8 existed here, then the "Wood" nature of the Southeast direction could cause even more domination of the 4-8 Flying Stars (Wood depleting Earth). Compare that to an 8-3 combination in the Northeast. With Northeast being an inherently "Earth" direction, the 8 Star will feel more comfortable in this direction.

Feng Shui practitioners can debate about the exact order or priority of influences with regards to the Flying Stars. What I have found is that the priorities are loosely as follows:

1. Mountain Star and Water Star

2. Annual Influences

3. Inherent Directional Element

4. Monthly Influences

This list does not include the ranking of the overall house types or the overlay of a Locked Period. But you can use common sense to come to your own conclusions. As an example, an 8-3 sector in a Reversed House is worse than an 8-3 sector in a Wang Shan Wang Shui House. And a 1-2 sector is worse during a Locked Period than without the Locked Period.

There are still more Stars not included in this book that can trigger certain events and circumstances, such as minor or "hidden" Stars that can affect specific things like construction projects.

After learning how to calculate the Flying Star charts and what the various combinations mean, the next step is to look at all the ways those imbalanced areas could be corrected and how the good combinations could be enhanced further.

Knowing how to use Five-Element theory properly is half the battle, explained in the previous chapters. But there are additional influences upon these unseen bundles of energies, which this next section will explain.

THE ELEMENTS IN A ROOM

After deciding what elements should be added to a room based on the productive, reductive, or destructive cycle, it is important to look at the existing room to decide what might need to be *taken away* from the room as well. Aside from adding water to a 4-7 room, it would also be advisable to remove excessive metal objects, since they would match the very element you are trying to reduce with water. You need to take an inventory of exactly what is in each sector (since they can span through several rooms) and *remove* the offending element or elements to the best of your ability. What if you cannot completely remove an offending element? Let us say that you have a brass bed frame in an 8-3 sector. Normally, this room should not have any Metal in it. But if you just can't part with the brass bed frame, then you just need to *add* more of the corrective element to compensate. I like to use the analogy that if someone wants to lose weight but refuses to reduce calorie consumption, then he or she has to add more exercise to see a result.

Does the building's construction material count for an element that may be required in a room? This is a really confounding situation. Let us say that a room needs Metal and the infrastructure behind the drywall is steel framing. Does this count? I cannot imagine that it would not count, but at the same time, you still need to control the qi in the room itself, so more Metal may be required. You have to have some metal exposed to the air in the room. Even metal objects under a bed will get some air flow.

What if there is a brick wall in a room that needs the Earth element? I would say that if the brick is exposed to the room's atmosphere and not covered up with drywall, then you have enough Earth represented by the exposed brick wall. It covers a large surface area, and the qi in the room can touch the earth. And on that note, does a kitchen that requires the Fire element need to have red dish towels or red-painted cabinetry? The answer to this lies within two circumstances. First, if the stove or oven is used daily, then it is probably not required to add additional fiery-colored objects to the room. Second, how much time is the occupant spending in the kitchen anyway? If a person is spending less than an hour per day in a kitchen, then it is not the most important room to remedy.

Some rooms are just a mixture of colors from the furnishings, fabrics, artwork, and wall paint. But if there is an element or color theme to the room, then it will have a big influence on the Flying Stars, and you will want to factor that into how or what you add to the room. Light, muted, or pastel colors are mostly harmless and therefore under the jurisdiction of personal, subjective taste. But a maroon wall is the Fire element, a blue wall is the Water element, a dark green wall is the Wood element, and bright yellow or orange walls are the Earth element.

FURNITURE VOLUME, HEIGHT, AND SHAPE

A room can be made "yin" or "yang" in part based on the type of furniture it contains. Big bulky pieces like desks or couches that are essentially too big for the room will make the room more "yin." If there is so much furniture that it impedes easy movement about the room, then the energy can become stagnant. Then, you have to look at the Flying Stars to make a projection about whether a yin environment is good or bad for those Flying Stars. For example: A 1-2 bedroom can make someone feel lonely or sickly, whether it is an empty room or filled to the brim. That is just the nature of the 1-2 Flying Stars. But if the actual décor of the room makes it more yin, then this is going to make the situation even worse. In general, excessively yin rooms can make people more somber, tired, or sickly while yang rooms can make people more active, lively, or extroverted. Of course, there always needs to be a balance of yin and yang for its own sake. Bedrooms can be more yin because sleeping is the number one activity in a bedroom. An office can, by definition, be more yang because you want to stir up more of the creative juices and assertiveness of the individual using the space.

To summarize: You want a balance of the volume of furniture in a room. Not too much and not too little, based on the room's dimensions and function. There is a subjective aspect to this as well. Some people feel more comfortable and cozy with a lot of things around them, whereas others feel more relaxed when the décor is sparse.

The volume of furniture in a room will affect the qi-flow, and that will affect the Flying Stars, too.

The size of the furniture affects the Flying Stars of the room in a way that many people will be surprised to read about. It may seem redundant after just discussing the volume of furniture because tall pieces, like bookshelves, just add to that total volume. But there is a difference between having the same cubic feet of furnishings all existing on a low level, such as couches or desks, as opposed to tall file cabinets, entertainment centers, or bookshelves. As discussed in the previous section, you can use furniture height to manipulate the Stars. Equally, lower furniture or lower floor levels can emulate a virtual type of Water. Continuing with the concept that everything affects everything, the shape of the furnishings and décor items can make the Flying Stars behave differently. Let's say we have a room with a lot of strong, straight lines and hard surfaces, lots of masculine chrome or steel. That is a very yang influence. Now, put that in a 7-6 or 6-7 sector, and it will just intensify things. If one definition of the 6-7 combination is "clashing swords" and that it can make people prone to arguing, then having very yang décor items will magnify the potential problem, especially if the décor items are the same literal element, such as sharp metal objects in a 6-7 room. Conversely, if you have a soft, denim-colored couch in a 6-7 room, the softer lines of the furniture and the blue color (weak Water) will help minimize the fighting nature of the Flying Stars. This is admittedly much more subtle than just adding or subtracting the raw elements to a room, but the shape of the furniture can either subdue or activate the Flying Stars.

The shape of the room itself is a factor, too. The 2-7 combination with a Period 9 Star creates an area that can trigger a fire. If the objects in the room or the room itself were a triangular shape, that would magnify the room's susceptibility to triggering an actual fire.

The 1-3 Flying Star pattern can stir up gossip. Put a round table in a room or have the 1-3 Flying Stars in a round entry hall and gossip will increase because round shapes make energies swirl around. Put an oscillating fan in this room and the gossip will really get activated. A spiral staircase can also swirl the energy.

OTHER YIN-YANG INFLUENCES

The 2-1 combination can make people depressed, so regardless of whether the room is full of furniture (more yin) or nearly empty (more yang), if the room is chronically dark, that will also exacerbate the negative. If the 2-1 room is bright and cheerful looking with plenty of natural light coming in, however, then that will help a little bit. You would still add Metal to the room. If you have a 3-2 area, which can cause arguments, exposed beams hovering overhead can make the situation worse.

So know that yin and yang environments will influence the Flying Stars in a predictable way. For example, if you have a fan blowing in a room that has the 3-2 combination, it will heighten the room's power to cause accidents. Light versus dark, still areas versus areas with a lot of commotion or activity, rooms that are typically quiet versus noisy will all affect the Flying Stars.

EXTERIOR INFLUENCES

A whole book can be devoted to exterior influences that impact people. Those exterior influences can have their own effect, regardless of whether there is a building, and then, of course, they can affect the qi in the building as well. For example, a dirty, stagnant body of water is not good Feng Shui under any circumstances. Then, if that dirty, stagnant water were near a house, it could compound the problems revealed in the Flying Star chart for the house. Some exterior influences are yin in quality, like a heavily forested area that casts a shadow on a house. Most exterior influences are yang in quality and stimulate the Flying Stars. Roads, streets, and highways will affect the Flying Stars if the house is relatively close to the street. A bright shining street light penetrating a window will bring the Fire element into a house. Nearby construction will cause vibrations to move toward a house, not unlike the way a nearby train can make a house actually shake. Just know that the outside will always affect the inside. This is one reason Feng Shui cannot be an exact science. We can't repeat the precise same interior and exterior environment with the same people in enough samples to test the repeatable outcome.

USE OF A ROOM

Within your own home, the rooms you use the most while awake are yang rooms, and the room you sleep in is a yin room. The exception would be for someone in a studio apartment where both yin and yang influences and activities converge. But whether you are sleeping, studying, exercising, eating, whatever you are doing in a room, it is the *amount of time you are exposed to the Stars* that will influence you predictably. If you have negative Stars in a guest room that you do not use, they will not affect you much.

The exception is the Flying Stars in the sitting, facing, or center sectors. These locations can affect the entire personality and qi of the house whether the rooms in those areas are used or not. If you own property that you do not live in, it will only affect you indirectly. For example, I help people purchase investment properties. If the property is Reversed Type, potentially bad for people and bad for money, then your tenants might have a hard time paying the rent sometimes. Or if there were accidents on the property because of the bad Feng Shui, the owner could be held liable. These are just a few things to consider, but the Feng Shui influence of property you do not dwell in should not affect you nearly as much as your own property.

THE PERSONAL TRIGRAM OF THE INDIVIDUALS USING A SPACE

The emphasis of this book is to teach you how to understand the potential effects of a house on anyone who lives there. For example, a 4-6 combination can similarly affect anyone with a leg or lower back problem. Once you factor in your own Personal Trigram (discussed in greater detail in *The Feng Shui Matrix*), however, it is understood that some people will be affected more than others by the same Star combination. This does not require an elaborate explanation. But here is one example: The 4-6 combination could trigger back or leg pain in anyone. It is the Qian 6 Metal Star dominating the Xun 4 Wood Star. If a Xun Trigram person occupies a room with the 4-6 combination, this person is more likely to be affected than someone who has a different

Personal Trigram. It is just one more layer. And with Feng Shui being a predictive art, if you know the Personal Trigram of the occupants, you can predict who is most likely to suffer or benefit from the Flying Stars in a home.

THE EAST/WEST SCHOOL

There is a branch of Feng Shui called the East/West school. This school caters to your best personal directions based on the year you were born and your gender. In addition, houses get categorized as being "east" type or "west" type based just on their sitting side and not their construction year. The East/West school is a simple branch of Feng Shui, and even though some practitioners use it exclusively, others practically abandon using its formulae once they learn the Flying Stars (Xuan Kong). Houses that *sit* in the West, Southwest, Northwest, or Northeast are called West-type houses. Houses that *sit* in the East, Southeast, North, or South are called East-type houses. Within each house type, there are four good locations and four bad locations that are consistent with these general categories. Within the West-type house, the locations of West, Southwest, Northwest, and Northeast are preferable to use over the easterly locations within the West-type house. In all of the East-type houses, the directions of East, Southeast, North, and South are going to be more positive areas based on this simplified diagnosis.

Below is an example of a house type chart based on this exact description. It sits in the West, facing East.

This simple way of looking at a house can present conflicts or discrepancies when compared to the Flying Star method. For example, in the West-sitting house, the location of Southeast is considered potentially negative. It is an easterly location within a westerly house. And yet, for many houses the Flying Stars in that sector will be very positive. This might be a 4-8 sector or a 6-1 sector in certain house types. *How do you reconcile which is more important or influential?* My experience is that the Flying Stars take precedence. They are more specific to the house you are evaluating because you are factoring in *time* as well as a more precise compass reading. Those who are trying to work with the East/West school are often frustrated by the limitations of four directions being good and four being bad for each of the eight house types. Master Sang once taught that you can improve the qi of the four bad directions with the element that nurtures the house type, *just as long as that element does not clash with the Flying Stars.* In order to use this formula for the East/West school, you have to know the Flying Stars so as not to have a remedy backfire on you. So, really, this technique is only for people who really want to use the East/West teachings in conjunction with the Flying Stars. You also need to know what element is productive to the house type (with the house type being defined by its sitting direction). Here is a chart that defines the house type and the element that supports that house type.

House Type Name	Sitting Side of House	Nurturing Element
Kan	North-Water	Metal
Gen	NE-Earth	Fire
Zhen	East-Wood	Water
Xun	SE-Wood	Water
Li	South-Fire	Wood
Kun	SW-Earth	Fire
Dui	West-Metal	Earth
Qian	NW-Metal	Earth

The chart above shows that a Li House is a "Fire" house in this formula. And Wood nurtures Fire. So, for the Li House, you can make the Northwest, West, Southwest, and Northeast sectors less negative by adding Wood (a live plant) to any of those sectors as long as it does not contradict what you would do with the Flying Stars in those same locations. Another example: If you have a Kun House, the locations of East, Southeast, South, and North will be negative areas according to the East/West school. Now, Fire strengthens the Earth house, so you can add a Fire remedy to any of those easterly directions within that house—*as long as Fire is not harmful to the Flying Stars in any of those areas.* You can continue to compare these two different schools for more layers of meaning. The specific impact of each direction in the East/West school is covered in greater detail in other books, including *The Feng Shui Matrix.* The same theory holds true for your best personal directions. If, based on your Personal Birth Trigram, you discover the direction of North is a bad direction for you personally, but if it is your bedroom and has the 8-6 Flying Stars, this bedroom will still be good for you. It just won't be as good for you as it would, in theory, for another person who does inherently well in the direction of North. Feng Shui is layers, layers, and layers.

CONCLUSION

Feng Shui has been practiced for several thousand years and has evolved over that time frame, with the information expanding along with the various styles of luo pans. No doubt it will continue to evolve and change.

There are no ancient Feng Shui texts that talk about Flying Star combinations that can cause car accidents, for example. But we can apply a modern interpretation to an ancient Flying Star predicament. Perhaps in the olden days the 3-2 combination meant that someone could be thrown off a horse as opposed to injured in an automobile accident.

There are no ancient Feng Shui texts that refer to a person having attention deficit disorder or chronic fatigue syndrome, and yet we can look at how the Flying Stars affect people in modern times and see a correlation. I once asked Master Sang what the 2-1 combination meant back in the days when people did not get divorced. He just smiled and said that a man would acquire a mistress. The same Flying Star combination that could indicate a prostitute (a woman who made money from her looks) in the olden days might very well boost the career of an aspiring model or actress in modern times.

So the Flying Stars, their meanings, and impact will continue to manifest in the very current ways we live. Just as the 5 Star can indicate a potential accident of any type, it can also indicate more frequent computer crashes if the 5 Star resides in your office.

And if the 3 Star at one time meant that your ship could be robbed by pirates, it might nowadays portend credit card fraud or identity theft.

The literal manifestations of the elements are changing, too. We have polluted air and water, depleted earth, and with global warming on the rise we cannot even count on having normal seasons and predictable weather patterns anymore. It does make me wonder whether the elements as remedies have lost some of their potency. But if everything is cyclical, as Feng Shui theory indicates, there will also be a time of purification, starting over, and new beginnings. If we think about our planet for a moment, it is large masses of earth and water. These are essential ingredients of life, earth and water. The Mountain Stars and Water Stars mirror that. Most of the circumstances surrounding us in life we have no control over. So it is comforting and intriguing to know that we can actually influence our own personal environment with these ancient principles and techniques. In your own life, and for the benefit of others, use the Feng Shui continuum as a blueprint for balanced living, now and in the future.

Kartar Diamond has been a leader in educating the western world about traditional Feng Shui since 1992. She received the bulk of her training from Master Larry Sang at the American Feng Shui Institute and has become one of the Institute's best-known graduates. She has published two previous Feng Shui titles, *Feng Shui for Skeptics* and *The Feng Shui Matrix*. Working with individuals and businesses in all phases, from land selection to design phase to existing properties, Kartar has advised thousands of clients, nationally and internationally. Her website, www.FengShuiSolutions.net, gives a full description of the various services she provides, including a free e-Newsletter. Aside from her busy Feng Shui consulting and teaching schedule, Kartar pursues other interests, including lyric writing, playing bass guitar, and practicing karate.

If you enjoyed reading *The Feng Shui Continuum*, be sure to get Kartar Diamond's other books.

Feng Shui for Skeptics: Real Solutions without Superstition

(2004) is a unique book in that it explains what is authentic Feng Shui versus the trendy and diluted versions of Feng Shui that sprang up in the 1990s and that are still perpetuated today. *Feng Shui for Skeptics* offers many case study examples of common house types and includes how to understand the yearly cycles of a house.

The Feng Shui Matrix: Another Way to Inherit the Earth

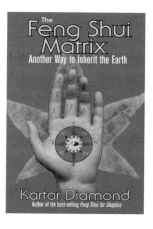

(2006) focuses on the personal applications and remedies that a person can utilize based on his or her birth year. It includes recommendations for how to have better relationships, health, and finances in ways that are unique to your own personal astrology. *The Feng Shui Matrix* also provides simple reference charts for how to determine the best and worst areas for Period 8 constructions.

These books are available on Amazon.com and directly through www.FourPillarsPublishing.com.

Give the Gift of
The Feng Shui Continuum
A Blueprint for Balanced Living
to Your Friends and Colleagues

CHECK YOUR LEADING BOOKSTORE OR ORDER HERE

❑ **YES**, I want _____ copies of *The Feng Shui Continuum*
$24.95 each, plus $4.95 shipping per book (CA residents: $2.06 sales tax per book)

❑ **YES**, I want _____ copies of *The Feng Shui Matrix*
$19.95 each, plus $4.95 shipping per book (CA residents: $1.64 sales tax per book)

❑ **YES**, I want _____ copies of *Feng Shui for Skeptics*
$14.95 each, plus $4.95 shipping per book (CA residents: $1.23 sales tax per book)

Canadian orders must be accompanied by a postal money order in U.S. funds. Allow 15 days for delivery.

❑ **YES**, I am interested in having Kartar Diamond speak or give a seminar to my company, association, school, or organization. Please send information.

❑ For a comprehensive consultation on your property, contact Kartar Diamond at 310-842-8870 or e-mail her at kartar@fengshuisolutions.net.

My check or money order for $_____ is enclosed.
Please charge my: ❑ Visa ❑ MasterCard

Name _____

Organization _____

Address _____

City/State/Zip _____

Phone_____ Email _____

Card # _____

Exp. Date_____ Signature _____

Please make your check payable and return to:
Four Pillars Publishing • 3824 Perham Drive • Culver City, CA 90232

Call your credit card order to: 310-842-8870
www.fengshuisolutions.net